Tales From The Rink

The Stories of the Players Who Made The Game Great

To John & Joann,

May your puck of life always find the net.

Best wishes

Tales From The Rink

The Stories of the Players Who Made The Game Great

by

Larry Nader

Copyright © 1999, 2000 by Lawrence P. Nader
All rights reserved.
This book may not be reproduced in whole or in part in any form or by any means, electronic or mechanical, including photocopying, recording or by any information storage system or retrieval system now known or hereafter invented, without the written consent of the author.

ISBN: 1-58820-118-X

1stBooks - rev. 9/26/00

ACKNOWLEDGEMENTS

In my years of following the game of hockey I have always admired the sacrifices made by the players and the families of those who play the game. Whether at a youth, junior, college or professional level, these families make sacrifices every day. From the mothers and fathers who get up at 4:30 every morning to take their future superstar to the rink for morning practices - which is usually the only time that teams can seem to get ice time - to the wives and children of these players who spend a good portion of their family life away from their husbands and fathers for the sake of the game.

It is to these families that I would like to extend my sincerest thanks and appreciation for helping to develop tomorrow's stars and keeping the dream alive. Without them and their dedication, hockey would have gone the way of the dinosaur, the Pony Express and the AMC Pacer.

Also, the coaches and other volunteers that work with our youngsters and help them advance in the game on their way to whatever level they finish playing at. There are a lot of fabulous people that dedicated their lives and time to helping our youth. Thank you all today for tomorrow's players.

I'd also like to thank each player that made time in his busy schedule to allow me the honor of interviewing him for this book. They have provided me, and I am sure all of you, with much enjoyment and many fond memories over the years – even those that I never had the chance to watch during their career. Thank you for allowing my readers and myself the chance to peek into your life up close and personal.

There have been many people, both in the hockey world and not, that befriended me in my endeavors to cover the game. It was their words of encouragement and praise that helped with the completion of this book. People like Brian Bierley, Blake Arnold, Steve Yuele, Mike Kitchen (not the ex-hockey player/coach, the other one that lives in Detroit under the guise of an accountant turning lawyer), and many others too numerous to mention here, helped me when the burnout of working a day job and writing for my own magazine, an internet magazine, and a book set in. They are truly teammates that you want on their bench when the puck drops.

I can't get out of here without thanking my family once again. Without their emotional and verbal support I would never have gotten to where I am today – after all I was a product of Detroit in the 1960s and 1970s. My mother Angela, my brothers Joe and Fred, sister-in-laws Sue and Rita, nephews Joe and Jim, my only niece and godchild Erica, my mother-in-law Joyce and father-in-law Warren were all there with encouragement, praise and support when I needed it most.

Last, but by no means least, the biggest thanks of all go to my wife of over 12 years Janis and our son Mikel. Many a time during my days publishing a struggling hockey magazine, as well as writing this book, I was ready to throw in the towel. Their encouragement, and an occasional boot in the ass when necessary, always got me back on track. Their refusal to allow me to walk away when things got their most stressful is the biggest reason that you are reading this book today. Mere thanks cannot express what they have meant to me over the years. Their love and support have gotten me through many a tough time and this book is as much theirs as it is mine.

Dedication

This book is dedicated to my best friend and loving wife Janis. Without her belief in my dreams, and me, this book might never have become a reality.

To my family and friends whose support and understanding has meant everything to me.

Also to all the players – past, present and future – that provide us with hours of true sports enjoyment and a diversion from our otherwise hectic lives.

TABLE OF CONTENTS

Acknowledegements v
Dedication vii
Preface xi
Bill Barber 1
Red Berenson 21
Robert Dirk 41
Bill Gadsby 57
Dennis Hextall 69
Larry Johnston 79
Nick Libett 95
John Ogrodnick 109
Pat Peake 127
Jimmy Peters, Sr. 139
Wayne Presley 153
Johnny Wilson 169

PREFACE

Hockey has traditionally been a game played predominately by men - tough men. And even as we enter the new millenium, though we find that women's hockey is starting to come into it's own, the professional ranks remain a male dominated sport.

Through the 1990's, the game of hockey saw a great increase in its marketability and, as a result, its popularity around the world. This increase was due in great part to the National Hockey League's attempt to marketing their product on a global basis.

On other levels, newer leagues like the United Hockey League, as well as the expansion of the East Coast Hockey League and International Hockey League, moved teams into markets yet untapped, helping spawn a new interest in a game that was previously thought only able to survive in the Northern United States and Canadian cities.

As the Canadian dollar weakened in the mid to late 1990's, and players salary demands increased, some of the Canadian markets once thought capable of supporting major-professional hockey found their teams moving south of the border. With this mini-exodus to the US, teams moved to markets that were once thought to only be able to support minor-professional teams at best.

The Winnipeg Jets packed up and headed to desert of Phoenix, Arizona and became the Coyotes; the Quebec Nordiques moved to Denver, Colorado and became the Avalanche – winning the Stanley Cup championship in their first year in their new city with a team built on Canadian fan support.

As the turn of the century approaches, Vancouver, Edmonton, Calgary and Ottawa are all said to be in financial turmoil and possible candidates to join their previously departed

Canadian franchise brothers in heading to where they feel they can generate enough revenue to support a profitable team.

All this movement, and marketing, has increased hockey fans desire for information on the stars that made the game what it is today.

While there have been many books that document the history of the game and the NHL, from its infancy to modern times, Tales From The Rink will provide you with insights into what these players of yesteryear went through on their climb to the top, their time there, and their life after the game.

Professional hockey players are among the toughest in any sport and arguable the best conditioned. Hockey isn't a game that you pick up at 15 years of age and join the pro ranks a few years later. It is a game of well-honed skills that takes 10, 15, or more years to perfect.

Through their young days growing up and playing the game strictly for the love of it, and then moving on to the professional ranks where they made their livelihood, you will hear the players own stories of how they came to achieve their level of success in the NHL.

These stories are told in their own words. Not an interpretation of what happened, but actual facts from the players themselves. I hope that you get as much enjoyment from reading Tales From The Rink as I did in writing it.

I wish to express my thanks to all the players featured in this book, for their time and insight into their lives. Many of these players were childhood idols of mine growing up in Detroit, Michigan, while others were players I came to enjoy watching in my adult life.

It has been said, "A hockey player never forgets, he just waits for the right opportunity to remember." As you'll be able to tell from these stories it doesn't matter how long they have been away from the game, they still remember all.

-- Lawrence P. Nader --
lpnad@mi.freei.net

Bill Barber

NHL Career: 1972-1984 (12 Seasons)
NHL Teams: Philadelphia Flyers
Hockey Hall of Fame Induction: 1990

You cannot think of the Philadelphia Flyers of the 1970's, (a.k.a. Broad Street Bullies), without thinking about Bill Barber. While he was never considered as one of the team's most ostentatious or pugilistic players, he was the type of backbone player that every championship team needs – the working man.

In 903 regular-season games with the Flyers, Barber racked up 420 goals and 463 assists for 883 points. He also appeared in 129 playoff games, scoring 53 goals and 55 assists while helping his club to two Stanley Cup Championships in 1974 and 1975.

During his playing career, Barber posted three seasons of 30+ goals, four seasons of 40+ goals and notched 50 lamplighters in the 75-76 campaign. In addition, he had the honor of playing on six NHL All-Star teams, as well as the 1979 Challenge Cup.

Barber spent time following his retirement as a coach and a scout in the Flyers' system, before winning the American Hockey League's Calder Cup as head coach of the Philadelphia Phantoms, the Flyers' farm club, in 1998. His #7 jersey is one of only four that have been retired by Philadelphia and hangs in the rafters at the team's First Union Spectrum home.

A BOYHOOD DREAM

William "Bill" Charles Barber was born in North Bay, Ontario on July 11, 1952 and raised in nearby Callander. As with any Canadian youth of the time, Barber lived for hockey, *playing it nearly every free moment he had. It was this drive and determination that led him to his successful career in professional hockey and two Stanley Cup Championships.*

Growing up in Callander, Ontario we had a community rink that my dad was instrumental in getting done for us. About the only thing we had back then (late 1950s and early 1960s) was that community rink. They dragged down an old schoolhouse in order to build an ice shack for us. They built the boards and gave us an opportunity, in what was really a rural area outside of Callander, to have some recreation. Obviously that recreation was hockey.

Back then the winters were somewhat colder than they are now and we had ice usually from the middle of November right on through to March. We were fortunate that way.

I lived above a service center, which my dad owned and operated, when I was 5-years-old. That was when I started skating. I then became involved with organized hockey around 6 or 7. Hockey was our recreation, especially after school and at night. Even on the weekends, all we ever did was skate. We would start early in the morning and, since I was fortunate enough to live close to this outdoor rink, I would also skate every night.

In 1961 my dad sold the service center and kind of semi-retired, so we had to move. He then built us a rink right next to our new house, that was regulation size and complete with lights. Besides benefiting us, it gave some of the people where we lived on this country road an opportunity for their kids to skate. As a result, I always had plenty of ice time.

Once I became involved in organized hockey I played for a small community called Wasi, which was a little community outside of Callander. It was not even big enough to be a town. We barely had enough kids to have a team. We had a goalie, 2 defensemen and 6 forwards. That was all we had. I played defense at the time along with a friend of mine and we would play the whole game, every game. We never came off the ice. It didn't matter whether we were in tournaments or regular games, we played the whole game.

That led on to each step that I made from pee wee to minor bantam to midgets and to junior. Back then we also didn't have many distractions. We didn't have VCR's, video games, computers or any of that other stuff. In the summertime we played some baseball and soccer, but that was about it. Hockey was *"The"* sport and the thing to do. It was also what I enjoyed most.

When I first started playing organized hockey I stayed within my age group, but as time went on I jumped up with some of the older kids. I missed a couple of age groups. I never played bantam at all. I went right from minor bantam to midget. When I was in midget, the kids I was playing with were high school kids and I was still in public school. I remember my dad driving me to early morning practices.

I almost bit off more than I could chew that year. I didn't have a bad year, but I had a tough one physically. I was obviously overmatched all the time with my opponents. That was a big learning process for me. From there I played a year of high school. That was beneficial. I think I grew a lot that year and had some good competition.

"From high school I went right into major junior as a 15-year-old in North Bay. I played then with a team called the Trappers, which are now the North Bay Centennials. They were in a league called the North Ontario Hockey Association (NOHA).

I was fortunate to get tied up with a great bunch of older guys (19-21 year-olds) in North Bay. There were only a few of us young guys on the team, so we really learned a lot that year. We had a chance to win a championship that year and I felt I made giant strides with them. It was probably the biggest advancement I ever had in my life as far as being a player goes. It was great to have a winning feeling and to win it all."

JUNIOR DAYS IN KITCHENER

Barber moved on to play his major-junior hockey with the Kitchener Rangers of the then Ontario Hockey Association, averaging over 100 points a year in two seasons there. The

Rangers, who drafted Barber in the OHA midget draft following his season with North Bay, helped him to continue to advance his game by moving him from defense to forward. As a result of his OHA success, the Philadelphia Flyers selected Barber with their first pick (7th overall) in the 1972 Amateur Draft.

The Kitchener Rangers of the Ontario Hockey Association drafted me in the 1969 Midget draft following my year in North Bay. The change from playing in North Bay to playing with Kitchener wasn't much. In the NOHA we were allowed a few 21-year-olds, so you grew up pretty quick. Obviously the caliber of hockey was better in Kitchener, but while our three lines in Kitchener were better than in North Bay, our better line in North Bay would have been able to compete in Kitchener. So it wasn't a big step, but it was a step in the right direction in order to improve as a player.

I started going to Kitchener's training camp as a 14-year-old and went there for three straight years before I was even drafted. My older brother played for the Rangers and they invited me to camp each year. Then when I became eligible in then midget draft they selected me. Since I had been at their training camps before it wasn't as big of an adjustment as it could have been. It worked out pretty well.

Kitchener is really a great town. It wasn't a city like Toronto, there was a little more warmth in the sense of where I came from. It was not real big and the fans were nice. The building was great to play in. We had some really good teams and I had a good line every year. We made real good progress as a team, as well as playing together as a line.

Unfortunately we didn't win a championship while I was there. We improved every year, but we fell a little short. However, I felt that the progress I made as a player, development-wise, worked out well for me. I really enjoyed playing there. I have a lot of great memories and friendships there that have lasted through the years.

I think that it was in my last year with Kitchener that we had a line called the "B-Line", which consisted of Jerry Byers (left wing), Albert Blanchard (right wing) and myself (center). We were all drafted in the top 12 in the 1972 NHL Amateur Draft – I went 7th, Blanchard was 10th and Byers was 12th. I think that is quit an honor. The Toronto line of (Billy) Harris, (Dave) Gardner and (Steve) Shutt were 1st, 4th and 8th respectively in that same year.

BREAKING IN WITH PHILLY

While he didn't start in immediately with the Flyers at the start of the 72-73 season, it took only 11 games with Philadelphia's farm team, the Richmond Robins, for Barber to hone his skills enough to get called up to the parent club as an injury replacement. Playing in 69 games that year for the NHL club, he tallied 64 points (30 goals, 34 assists) while playing on Bobby Clarke's wing. The Flyers only lost six games that season when Barber scored a goal.

I always felt confident that I could play in the NHL. The reason I did was that I had played against some of the New York Ranger players already. Walter Tkaczuk and Vic Hatfield and a few other players dropped in with our training camp in Kitchener because they had contract problems. So I had a chance to compete against them as a junior. As a result of the experience, I felt really comfortable that I could play at that level.

Montreal had the 4th, 6th and 8th picks that year and I went between all of that. When Philly drafted me I was pleased because I knew I had a chance of maybe stepping in that year and playing. I couldn't have been any happier with the situation and the way it worked out.

"I went into camp with Philly that first season and had an alright camp, but it wasn't a camp that I was happy with. I had a hard time making some adjustments, and as a result spent a few games in the minors. After 11 games with Richmond I was called up and, once I got my feet wet, I felt really comfortable with my role. They put me on wing and I felt right at home with the players I was lined with.

I had an exciting first year of pro and was very comfortable with my role. We went to the semi-finals that year and things went from there where we had the opportunity to win a couple of championships. It was a case of the right people at the right time.

I was playing with the Richmond Robins in Hershey, Pennsylvania when I was called up to the Flyers. We were getting ready to head back to Richmond when the Flyers assistant coach Mike Michaluk, who happened to live in Hershey, came down after the game and told me I was going up to the Flyers as an injury replacement. They were playing against Toronto at the Spectrum in Philadelphia so I headed to Philly and never went back. It took me about three or four games to get going and thank God that Fred Shero had the patience to keep putting me in there. He gave me a chance to get things going.

The first few games I was just a player. Then, in a game I remember vividly against Buffalo, I got a couple of goals and a couple of assists and things started to fall into place. I knew I finally broke the ice and it really helped my confidence. Then as time went on I was placed into some special team roles, which I responded well to.

Fred Shero was more of a father image to me since I was only 20 years old at the time. My brother had played for Shero in the minor leagues with Omaha and Buffalo, and I remember him saying to me that I was going love playing for him. He said, 'If you can't play for him, you can't play.' It was as simple as that and he was right. He was a great guy to play for and he gave me every opportunity to excel career-wise. He put me with good players immediately.

When I was first called up I was put right on the line with (Gary) Dornhoefer and (Rick) MacLeish. After a little time I ended up on a line with Clarkie (Bobby Clarke) and Bill Flett. He put me with good players and really gave me a chance to raise my level of play so that I felt comfortable. Then, in time he put me on the power play as a defenseman. So I really owe him a lot. I just found it difficult not to play hard for that man.

I think a lot of our schooling was done within the dressing room at the time as well. We had some great leadership with guys like Clarkie, Ed Van Impe, Joe Watson and Barry Ashbee.

They made sure you were ready to play and if you weren't on top of your game you heard about it. When you are a young player it is important to have guys believe in you.

It was a special kind of a team that was young but blended with some older guys that had won and paid the price. We went on to win back-to-back championships. That feeling is still hard to replace, as far as enthusiasm within the city goes.

BROAD STREET BULLIES

The mid-1970's belonged to the Philadelphia Flyers and it was their tenacious play and unwillingness to lose that helped earn them the nickname of "Broad Street Bullies",[1] as well as a pair of championships. While it was a title that was placed on them by the hockey media, it was also one that struck fear into many an opposing player.

Players like Dave Shultz, Gary Dornhoefer and Ed Van Impe did their best to use the reputation in their favor - especially Shultz who posted 1386 penalty minutes in a mere 297 games with Philly. To this day, many of the players of that era talk about their teammates coming down with mysterious ailments that only seemed to happen when it came time to play the Flyers. Barber, however, feels the nickname was somewhat exaggerated by overzealous hockey writers of the era.

In my own opinion, I think the Broad Street Bullies thing kind of got out of hand. I don't think that we were a goon team, we just played hard and wouldn't accept losing. We had a lot of talented and hard working guys on the team, and that was overshadowed because of that nickname. The writers wrote what they thought would sell.

Sure we were a rugged team and possibly the toughest team in the league, but there were other teams in that era like Boston and St. Louis that had tough teams as well. I think, in our

---

[1] The media coined the name Broad Street Bullies due to the Flyers rough style of play and the arena they played in, the Spectrum, being located on Broad Street.

situation, it was exaggerated and the talent was overshadowed because of it.

Even though we were talented, we didn't have a lot of flash. We just had guys that would pay the price and work hard. We had one goal when we stepped onto the ice and that was to win. It started with our goaltending. We had great goaltending and a solid defense. On top of that, we had three lines that could compete with any three lines in the league at the time. As a whole, we played a style that gave us a chance to stay in every game and win.

We were a stay at home kind of team and won low scoring games by one goal. Everyone bought into the system and, I think, when you have that you have a chance to win championships. The leadership, and the commitment by all of the players to accept their roles was vital to our success."

STANLEY CUPS I & II

Many players retire from the game with only dreams and near chances of wining a Stanley Cup. Barber considers himself honored to have earned the right to drink from Lord Stanley's silver chalice twice. The 6' 0", 195-pound Barber was an integral part of Philly's success during the mid-70's, helping them to consecutive Cup celebrations in 1974 and 1975.

Everyone on the team was happy. It was an exciting time. We just wanted to play and win for the city of Philadelphia. We had a great team and great fan support. Once we won the first Stanley Cup, it all came out as far as the backing we had from the city. It was fabulous.

We had been to the semifinals in 1973 and had given Montreal all they could handle, so this wasn't a complete surprise to us when we got there. Maybe for some of the fans and hockey people we were a bit of a surprise to get to the finals, but that was not the case in our minds. We knew we were close and just needed to make a few fine adjustments.

We won our first Stanley Cup in game 6 of the finals in 1974 against the Boston Bruins. We beat them 1-0 that game to win the Cup. It was a special moment. It was the game that got us established as champions. It was extra special that we were able to go on and win it again in 1975 against Buffalo.

It was an excellent experience for me, as it would be for any young player, to get to the semifinals once and win two Stanley Cups in my first three years as a professional.

Both Championships were won in game 6. We defeated Boston on our home ice and Buffalo on theirs. The second year was as enjoyable as the first, if not more so. With the experience of winning the Cup in the previous year, I was able to control my emotions better and really absorb what was going on.

Both Cups were exciting, but different. Winning at home had more energy since the fans had a chance to see us win the championship for the first time. We had only been in existence since 1967 and in a short period of time we were Stanley Cup Champions. I am really glad that first one happened at home. You couldn't have asked for a better situation.

That second year, however, it was great for us as players to win on the road. All of our dads were in for the game and we had a chance to enjoy the celebration with them. It was also important that we had a chance to celebrate as a team before chartering back to Philly. It was nice to have our own little private time.

The welcoming we got at the celebration parades was great both years. The first year there was over 1 million people and the second year over 2 million turned out. I think that speaks for itself. The people in Philadelphia are really great hockey fans and we loved to win for them.

THOSE PESKY RUSSIANS

Many of you may vividly remember that 1975-76 season when two Soviet Union teams (Central Red Army and Soviet Wings) traveled through North America playing an eight-game series against selected NHL teams. It was a time when fans across Canada, and the United States alike, had to face the realization that their homegrown players may not any longer be the best in the world.

The Russians swept through the NHL cities leaving a string of defeated NHL clubs in their wake. They were yet to be beaten heading into their contest against the Flyers, as the NHL teams could manage no more than a single tie.[2] The Russian's quickly found out why the Flyers had been dubbed the Broad Street Bullies.

The Soviet team was on tour that year and had not lost a game, and their only tie was with Montreal. The game was televised around the world and it really put a lot a lot of pressure on our team to win, which I thought was healthy. We were one of the better teams in the league and we wanted to show that to the world.

In my opinion, it was a pretty lopsided game. We outshot them 40-something to 15 and our scoring chances were probably 7-1 or 8-1, which for that era of hockey that was pretty phenomenal.

We played our systems well. They had a lot of the puck control during the game but Fred Shero did a great job to prepare us for their style and we knew what to expect. While the Russians feasted on puck control, we feasted on dumping it in, chasing it down and hunting the puck. I think that was a big factor in the game's outcome.

We would keep putting the puck in their end but (Russian netminder Valdislav) Tretiak never came out to stop it. That always gave us an opportunity to get the puck back. Their system was to enter the zone with speed and puck control. Our defensive system was pretty tough to penetrate and they kept turning the puck over. Sooner or later someone was bound to make a mistake.

Obviously the memorable part of the game was the hit by Ed Van Impe on one of their players, I'm not sure which one it was. Eddie had come out of the penalty box at the time and was bee-lining it back to our zone, as the Russians were on the attack at the time. Van Impe caught the Russian player (Valery

---

[2] The NHL's only non-loss over the Russian's prior to that day came on New Year's Eve in Montreal when the Canadiens managed a 3-3 tie.

Kharmalov) with his head down, laying him out. He didn't get up and that kind of set the tone as their team walked off the ice. Things were finally worked out with the Russian team and they came back out to finish the game.

A little while after we got the game going again, we went on the power play. I shot the puck from the point and Reggie Leach tipped it past Tretiak giving us a 1-0 lead. From that point on the game was over.

I thought our team handled the pressure well. We were prepared to play but you are never guaranteed anything just for being ready. Then on the other hand, we dealt with the pressure of the importance of us winning this game – one game – very well. It was like the Super Bowl, winner takes all.

We helped save face for all of North American hockey and the guys were proud of that. I thought it was a lopsided game and our guys couldn't have executed a better game plan than we did that game."

THE CANADA AND CHALLENGE CUP TEAMS

In addition to his other accolades, Barber was selected to represent his native country of Canada in the '76 and '81 Canada Cups. He was also selected as a player for the '79 Challenge Cup, which replaced the league's annual All-Star event that year.

The 1976 Canada Cup was the first time that athletes at this level were assembled from six countries for a hockey tournament, outside of the Olympics. Barber's Canadian squad, who hosted the event, proved victorious over Czechoslovakia, Finland, the Soviet Union, Sweden and the United States.

It is always a great honor whenever you get a chance to represent your country in competition. You always gain experience from it. We had been to the finals three times and now there was the Canada Cup. We really had some fun with it.

I had a chance to play on the same team with Bobby Hull, Phil Esposito, Guy Lafleur and guys that I watched growing up. It's a great opportunity to be thrown in with players of that caliber. The concept in 1976 was different from 1972 when Team Canada played games in both Canada and Russia in an eight game Super-Series between the two countries. In 1976 there were six teams in the tournament, not just the two.

We ended up playing the Czechoslovakian team for the Cup that year. I couldn't have been any happier with the outcome and the experience I gained. The whole event was first class from start to finish and it was a big commitment from the guys.

Barber's selection to the 1979 Challenge Cup team was just one of six All-Star game appearances that he would earn. While honored to play in the event, he feels it was a mistake by the NHL to schedule this series in the middle of the year and expect a team that had never played together before to perform at an international level of play.

The 1979 Challenge Cup was thrown into the middle of the NHL season. I don't think the timing was great. We didn't have great success and lost out in the last game. Putting a team together in such a short period of time halfway through the season, where injuries and fatigue were involved, wasn't such a good idea.

You have to understand that the European teams gear for these tournaments. We were playing for a living and our schedule was very demanding in the sense of travel and amount of games played. I don't think there was any advantage to play at that time of the year.

It's not an excuse. The facts are the facts. It was a great experience, but unfortunately we didn't win. What it did do though was to generate more interest in the game.

Then in 1981, Barber was selected to represent Canada once again in international play. However this time he was unable to play in the Canada Cup series because of a knee injury suffered in the team's last practice before the start of the tournament.

I was fortunate enough to be selected for the Canada Cup once again in 1981. While I was getting down near the end of my career, they had confidence in my ability to come in and play. I had a good camp, but unfortunately in the very last intersquad game I sprained my knee. The injury put me out for the tournament.

I watched the series very closely and felt for the guys. They didn't have success in that tournament and I felt even worse because I wasn't able to be there. It's not that any one person could have made a difference, because I don't believe that would have been the case, but I wish I was there even with the outcome the way it was.

Fortunately I was able to get back in time to start the season with Philadelphia after missing all of training camp. Missing the Canada Cup gave me a better chance to work out with the Flyers conditioning guy and getting myself back mentally and physically. So it worked out for the best.

CUTTING THE LACES

As a result of several knee injuries in his career, Barber underwent surgery following the 83-84 season. The extent of the damage to his knee eventually forced him to retire from the game. His goal scoring statistics were so impressive that he remains the franchise's leading scorer to this day, while he places second in points and games played, and third in assists. Having played only 12 seasons in the NHL, his decision to retire was not an easy one.

I really believed that I could have played for an extended period of time. Back then, playing 12 years in the NHL was maybe an average career, or a little less. But I really believed that from the way I felt, my body structure, and the way I could skate that I could have played longer.

I could have possibly moved back and played on defense. I played defense all my life as a young kid. I didn't play forward until I started playing in Kitchener. I guess they figured that since I was up the ice all the time anyway, they'd just move me there. But I grew up as a defenseman and felt I could have enjoyed a few more seasons in that position.

Even in the pros, I always played the point on the power play. I played defense for Pat Quinn when he was with the Flyers. We had run into injury problems and were short defensemen, so I moved back to defense and played there for a bit. I always felt comfortable on defense.

If I was healthy, I felt that I could have kept playing and not just have been a body out there. Maybe my role would have been cut back, which is understandable due to the youth movement, but I could have contributed and helped the younger guys out. Unfortunately that was not the case.

My knee had been banged on a couple of times during my career, to the point where I had extensive damage to it. The only way to get it back was to do major re-constructive surgery. What really set me back career-wise is that it wasn't just the ligaments that were damaged. It turned out that once they got inside the knee they found that I had bone damage to my femur (the large bone in your leg that runs into the knee joint). It turned out that there was a square inch of bone torn off of that, which we were not aware of. We didn't have MRI's back then and they couldn't really tell the extent of the damage until they opened me up. When they did it looked like a bomb had gone off in there.

The surgery was scheduled to be a 3 ½ hour procedure, but it quickly became 5 hours with what they found. At that point my career was in trouble. I knew that just by them opening my knee up, and the extent of the damage found, that I was going to have a long road to haul just to make it back to be able to carry on with a normal life.

I rehabilitated the knee for a year following the surgery, hoping to make a comeback. We didn't make any announcements at all about my status, I figured we would just see how it went. I worked hard for a solid year to rehab the knee, but I never got my full range of motion back. As a result, I was unable to continue playing and had to consider retiring.

FROM COACHING TO SCOUTING AND BACK AGAIN

Realizing the value of the hockey knowledge he had gained over the years, the Philadelphia management quickly approached Barber about coaching opportunities within the club. Accepting the offer, Barber and was named head coach of the team's American Hockey League affiliate Hershey Bears before moving up as an assistant coach with the Flyers. From there Barber transferred to scouting, serving as the club's Director of Pro Scouting from 1988 to 1996.

While I was going through my rehabilitation period, I went to Hershey and coached our American League farm team for their last 14 games of the 1984-85 season. I was given the opportunity to stay onboard with Hershey, but my family was young and I wanted to stay in the Philly area. So I moved back to the Flyers becoming an assistant coach working on player development under Mike Keenan, who was the head coach at the time.

While I was an assistant coach I had been doing some follow-up work with our junior players to make sure that things were moving along as they should be in the young player's career. So from there I moved into scouting for the team.

I believe we were the first team to start scouting players at the professional level. I was in charge of scouting strictly pro games – no junior or college games. The Flyers were finding out that trades were beneficial, and necessary, in order to win, and you needed to have your own personnel's input concerning the trades.

I covered the National, American and International Hockey Leagues, which was really a large chunk to cover. I was always on the go from September until the end of April and sometimes the first part of May. I would take in between 145 to 160 games a year. I was really on the go. I usually only had the odd Monday off during that time. I think that the longest I ever went without a break, while I was scouting, was 24 straight games in

24 nights. That was in February of 1995, following the work stoppage.

It was tough with having a family and being gone so much. It seemed like I was always on the road. It is a lot worse than being a player. Playing was the easy part. Those are the best times of your life. All you had to worry about was your own play, and staying focused.

On December 30, 1995, Barber returned to Hershey finishing the season with the Bears as head coach once again. The team was relocated the following season to Philadelphia, taking the moniker of the Phantoms. Barber has been instrumental in the success of the First Union Spectrum's other team, leading the Phantoms to the AHL's Calder Cup Championship in 1998.

I returned as head coach of the Hershey Bears in December 1995 and then followed the franchise back to Philadelphia when we became the Phantoms. 1996-97 was our inaugural year in Philly and we had a great year.

The Flyers gave us a really solid hockey team that first season, but we fell a little short. The following year (97-98) we kept building and the guys marched us right to a championship. Our fan base in Philly is really second to none in the American League.

Barber's Phantoms won their first Calder Cup championship on home ice at the Spectrum in front of a record sellout crowd of 17,380 by defeating the St. John Flames in six games - coincidentally the same number of games that won the Flyers their two Cups in the mid-1970's.[3]

Winning the Calder Cup was an experience that I will never forget. The building was sold out. The fan following was great

---

[3] The Phantoms also became the first team in AHL history to draw over 100,000 fans in a playoff season, topping out at 106,641.

and the media coverage was unreal. We hit every front page of every local paper around. I am very proud of that ring.

Barber has seen professional Cup Championships on both sides of the fence – 2 Stanley Cups as a player and 1 Calder Cup as a head coach. For Bill the taste of the champagne in each of those cups was just as sweet.

The victories are equally sweet, but as a coach it is probably more rewarding, due to the elements that you battle through. There are a lot of major sacrifices you make to win a championship as a head coach. As a player I think you focus in on what you need to do to win, where as a coach you are responsible for 20-plus players and all the other things that go along with it.

It was sweet. I really enjoyed it. I set a goal to hopefully win another championship at this level and if I get an opportunity to coach in the NHL, which I am hoping will be the case down the line, my major objective is to win a Cup at that level too. Then, all of my dreams would have come true.

We have a real good main core of guys that compete hard every night. I think it is important to express to the players the necessity of tradition and pride of an organization, as well as the history of the Spectrum building itself and what it represents to the city. I stressed strongly during the inaugural year that we had to maintain a high level of play and be a committed team that worked hard and never quit. No matter what the situation was on the ice, winning or losing, we had to play hard for our fans. If we want to put people in the building, we have to play, and play hard.

We are very honored and privileged to be playing in a building that has hoisted two Stanley Cups. The least we can do is maintain a high level of play and try to win a championship. So far we have done all that and we will continue to try to do it again.

BEING INDUCTED

One of the biggest highlights of Barber's career is his induction into hockey's most illustrious of institutes – The Hockey Hall of Fame. His induction in 1990 came only a year following his selection into the Flyers' Hall of Fame.

Being inducted into both the Flyers Hall of Fame and the Hockey Hall of Fame were great honors. I think anytime you are recognized in a Hall of Fame situation, it is an honor and something to be proud of.

I look at it, in my situation, as it is representative of the players I played with. I wasn't the flashiest guy on the ice. I played the game because I loved to play. I loved to win and compete, and I had some great players surrounding me that helped me do that. When I was inducted to the Hockey Hall of Fame, I acknowledged that. I thanked all my teammates because they were a big part of getting me there.

You are only as good as your hockey team. It is not a one-man show. What more can you ask for than to play a game you love. You play hard and the reward at the end of it all is to leave the game with championships and Hall of Fame inductions. I can't say more than that.

Bill Barber's Career Stats

Season	Team	League	GP	G	A	Pts	PIM
1972-73	Richmond Robins	AHL	11	9	5	14	4
1972-73	Philadelphia Flyers	NHL	69	30	34	64	46
1973-74	Philadelphia Flyers	NHL	75	34	35	69	54
1974-75	Philadelphia Flyers	NHL	79	34	37	71	66
1975-76	Philadelphia Flyers	NHL	80	50	62	112	104
1976-77	Philadelphia Flyers	NHL	73	20	35	55	62
1977-78	Philadelphia Flyers	NHL	80	41	31	72	34
1978-79	Philadelphia Flyers	NHL	79	34	46	80	22
1979-80	Philadelphia Flyers	NHL	79	40	32	72	17
1980-81	Philadelphia Flyers	NHL	80	43	42	85	69
1981-82	Philadelphia Flyers	NHL	80	45	44	89	85
1982-83	Philadelphia Flyers	NHL	66	27	33	60	28
1983-84	Philadelphia Flyers	NHL	63	22	32	54	36
	NHL Totals		**903**	**420**	**463**	**883**	**623**

Red Berenson

NHL Career: 1961-1978 (17 Seasons)
NHL Teams: Montreal Canadiens, New York Rangers, St. Louis Blues, Detroit Red Wings

Over the years, Red Berenson has proved himself to be a winner at the collegiate and professional levels of hockey, as both a player and coach. After a successful college career with the University of Michigan Wolverines (1959-62), in which he was a three-year varsity letter winner, Berenson moved on to the NHL where he had continued success.

While with the Wolverines, Berenson set a school record with 70 points (43-27) in a mere 28 games. His 43 goals and nine hat tricks in his final season remains a University benchmark to this day.

In 1962, after leading Michigan to second place in the WCHA, Berenson helped Michigan to third place at the NCAA Championships. He then played for the Montreal Canadiens the very next night in a game at the Boston Gardens becoming the first collegiate player to step right into the NHL.

Overall, Berenson played 17 seasons in the NHL including being a part of the Montreal Canadiens' 1964-65 Stanley Cup Championship team. In addition to Montreal, Berenson spent time with the New York Rangers, St. Louis Blues (two tours of duty) and Detroit Red Wings. In 987 NHL games played, he tallied 261 goals with 397 assists.

In May 1984, he became the fourth former U-M captain to take over the coaching reigns of his alma mater when athletic director Don Canham appointed Berenson to the position. Stepping behind the bench, Red took over the task of putting together a solid hockey program at Michigan that has been responsible for graduating numerous players to the NHL ranks.

In addition, Berenson turned the Michigan hockey program into the winningest hockey program in the 1990's. Michigan brought home their first NCAA championship in 32 years under Berenson's tutelage in 1995-96, and followed it up with another in 1997-98.

EARLY YEARS

Born in Regina, Saskatchewan in 1939, Gordon "Red" Berenson, like most prairie-land Canadian kids, first started skating at the ripe old age of 2. Little did Red's mother know when she took him out for that first time, where it all would lead.

I grew up in Regina, Saskatchewan, which was a pretty good size city - about 100,000 in population at the time. We didn't have sidewalks, running water or electricity in the West End when I was a kid. Eventually we got electricity, but I don't remember when we got running water. It was a severe winter climate there and the culture was hockey.

With the weather, everyone played hockey outside on natural-ice rinks. There was a water tap down the street and we would let it run until we filled up the corner lot, and we'd have ice. It didn't seem to matter how cold it was, or if there was a blizzard, we'd be out there playing shinny hockey with skates on, or off.

Back in the 1940's there was no television, so we would listen to hockey games on the radio. We would get the Toronto games, so everyone was a Maple Leaf fan. I have pictures of when I was three or four getting a Maple Leafs' jersey for Christmas. How proud I was of that jersey.

I also remember my best Christmas, when I got a pair of hockey gloves and fiber shin pads. What a great thing that was.

All my friends played hockey and I played along with them. I started skating when I was 2. My mother got me out on the prairie rink and I learned from there. Then, when I was 12, we moved a little further west in town where we had an outdoor rink right across the street. It had boards and lights, so we were able to play hockey literally all night, every night. You would come home from school and go play in games or referee. You'd be on the ice all the time.

On the weekends, and even when the rink was closed, we would shovel it off and play pick-up hockey all day. I'd come home for supper with my skates and equipment on, sit down, eat and be gone again. It was not only a pastime it was a passion. There was no thought about not playing hockey. If you didn't play hockey, you didn't fit in.

We had a parks league that was organized by the city, through the schools. You didn't play for your school team, you played for different teams depending on where you lived. I lived near rink #11. All the rinks had numbers.

Each year, as you got older, you'd play at a different level. When you became a better player, you could try out for the Regina Pats' teams. They had teams that played once a week at an indoor rink called Regina Stadium. It was a big thing to play at an indoor rink, but you had to be at least bantam age. We played games there every Saturday.

I liked it so much, that I decided I wanted to skate there more often. So, I'd have my mother get me up at five o'clock in the morning and I'd be at the rink before 6 a.m. I would sneak in through a window that I knew I could open and be skating in there when the janitor showed up and turned the lights on. He'd ask me how I got in and I would tell him the door was open.

They picked an all-star team at the end of the year from all the teams that competed in the league and I was lucky enough to make the team when we played for the Provincial championship. Our Regina Pats' teams were good and typically produced the Province champions.

Eventually you played on the junior team. That was major-junior hockey and by then the Montreal Canadiens owned you. They didn't have a draft then, they owned the territorial teams. So if you played for Regina, Montreal owned you.

As a young player I ended up being named Rookie of the Year my first season. In my second year, I was on the first All-Star team and we had a good year. I still had two more years of junior eligibility, but by then I had finished high school. So I decided to go to college.

DOING IT HIS WAY

The road Berenson chose on his way to the NHL was a very tough one. After talking with coaches and older players, he opted to play college hockey at the University of Michigan, instead of continuing in major-junior hockey. While he was aware that getting to the NHL from the U.S. College system was nearly impossible, he was aware of the need for a good education in case his hockey career didn't pan out.

I talked to some ex-professional players and they told me, 'There are only six teams in the NHL. If you are going to make it, you'll make it. But be sure to get an education.' That was the one thing that most of them regretted.

The Montreal Canadiens told me, 'You'll never be a pro if you go to school.' They did everything to try to convince me not to go. But my mind was made up. I decided that I would go to the University of Michigan and still try to play pro.

At the time, Murray Armstrong coached Denver University. He had been the major-junior coach with the Regina Pats. Everyone respected and admired him. When he left and took the college job, he recruited a lot of players to go with him. I was just coming up then, but I saw that happen.

Two of the schools that were interested in me were Denver and North Dakota. After that Michigan got involved. The deciding factor in my choice was that Michigan was the best school academically. I visited there and saw that it was a big school and it was near Detroit, which had NHL hockey. I had never seen a NHL hockey game before. They (Michigan) asked me if I wanted to be a big fish in a small pond or a big fish in a big pond. I decided that I wanted to be a big fish in a big pond.

Al Renfrew was the coach at Michigan at the time. He was a great person and had coached at other schools. He had played his hockey at Michigan, but was from Toronto. Al was a big influence on me in terms of coming to Michigan and getting the most out of college hockey, as well as getting the most out of school.

There were five of us from the Regina team that came down to play for Michigan, so I was fortunate to have some people I knew on the team. Then the following year we recruited about four or five more from Regina. At that point the program started to take off.

Back then you couldn't play your first year in college. So, during my first season, I just practiced. However, we played a game against the Detroit Red Wings every year, and I was eligible to play in that. I also played in a scrimmage game against the Toledo Mercurys of the International Hockey League. Outside of that we just practiced.

After Christmas, the Belleville MacFarlands, who were representing Canadian in the World Tournament, asked me to come along as an add-on. They had been the Allan Cup champions for senior teams in Canada, and they recruited a few young players to join their team for the tournament, so I decided to go.

I left school and we played all over Europe. We played in Scotland, Norway, Sweden, Finland, Switzerland, Germany, and Italy. We eventually played in the finals in Czechoslovakia and won the tournament, which was a pretty big thing. To beat the Russians at that time (in 1959) was a great thrill. They were good even back then.

When I came back, the Canadiens kept me in Montreal for a couple of days. I guess my stock went up while I was in the tournament and they wanted me to sign right then. However, I felt loyal to Michigan, and I went back to play the next three years.

My last year of college hockey (61-62), we were in the NCAA Final Four. We had a good team but we didn't win. After that last game in the tournament, Ken Rearden, who was the Vice President of Montreal, drove me to Boston and we negotiated a contract. The next night I was playing for Montreal at the Boston Gardens.

ON TO THE PROS

Berenson's leap to the National Hockey League was instantaneous. In the spring of 1962 he went from playing in the NCAA tournament for the University of Michigan to playing the last four games of the regular season for the Montreal Canadiens, making him the first player to make it directly to the NHL from the American College route.

The Red Baron, as Berenson was nicknamed, split the next season between the Canadiens and their minor pro affiliate the Hull-Ottawa Canadiens, in the Eastern Professional Hockey League. Berenson played a total of 136 games with Les Habitants in a little over four seasons, before being traded to the New York Rangers.

It (getting to the NHL) was a great thrill for me. Not just because I did it my way, but because I did it the right way. I came back to Michigan after Montreal was eliminated from the playoffs in 1962, to finish my studies and graduate from Michigan's business school in three and a half years. Even though American College hockey was frowned upon then, I was able to continue to improve and develop well enough to step into the NHL right out of college.

After I made it to the NHL directly from college, other players like Tony Esposito, Keith Magnuson, Cliff Koroll, Bill Masterton, Lou Angotti, and a long list of others, followed. There was a bit of a trend there, but it has taken a long time for the pros to recognize that college hockey players are just as good as, if not better than, those playing junior hockey. I really believe that this is the way to go for a kid that is capable of getting an education.

I was up and down with Montreal. It was hard to break in then. Montreal was a great team then, and they only dressed five defensemen and 11 forwards. They played three lines. So there were two forwards that didn't play much. I was one of those two.

After 20 games in the 62-63 season, they weren't playing me much so I was sent down to Hull-Ottawa, their farm club. I did very well there. Scotty Bowman was the assistant coach and Sam Pollock was the head coach. Montreal had some great players in Hull-Ottawa at that time – like Jacque Laperriere, Bobby Rousseau, Terry Harper and Jimmy Roberts – that all eventually played in the NHL.

I was up and down a lot. Whenever they needed me I'd go up, but I wouldn't play much. It was kind of frustrating not to play much of a role up there. The next year I felt that I had a pretty good idea of what they wanted and stuck around for the whole year, even though I still received somewhat limited playing time. You would kill penalties or fill in for someone if they got hurt, but other than that you didn't play much. That year, Bryan Watson and I were the two extra players and we had a lot of fun together.

Montreal was a special place to play. At that time, there was no team in the league that you would rather play for than Montreal. Rocket Richard had just retired the year before I got there, but (Jean) Beliveau, (Henri) Richard, (Bernie) Geoffrin, (Dickie) Moore and (Jacques) Plante were all there. Doug Harvey had just been traded. Toe Blake was the head coach at that time, and he was very successful.

It was a great tradition there and you really felt it. Every day I would step on the ice for practice and it was like magic. I couldn't believe I was there. Even though I wasn't very successful in Montreal, I was appreciative to be playing for the Canadiens. I know that times have changed, because people don't always say that anymore. But at that time it was something special.

ON THE RANGE

During the summer of 1966, Berenson was dealt to the New York Rangers in return for Ted Taylor and Gary Peters. Once in New York, he spent most of the season on the injured list and never really recovered enough to prove his worth. Playing in just 49 games for the Rangers over two seasons, Berenson managed only 2 goals and 6 assists, prompting New York to trade the slow starting scorer.

I was traded to New York in the summer of 1966. The NHL Entry Draft was a couple of years away but they still had a protected list and Montreal would trade players so that they wouldn't lose them.

I think it could have been good for me, but it just didn't work out. When I got to New York, Emile Francis was the coach and manager. He gave me every opportunity to play there and it looked like things were going to go well. However, early in the season I broke my big toe and I kept playing on it because I didn't want to lose my spot. Pretty soon I couldn't even skate and had to sit out for a while.

My first game back, on Christmas night, (Eric) Nesterenko caught me with an elbow and broke my cheekbone. So now I was out for another few weeks and when I came back I had to wear a mask to protect my face. By then our team was playing really well and breaking back into the line-up was hard. It turned out to be my worst season in hockey.

I told the Rangers that I didn't think it was working out and I wanted to go somewhere else. The next season was the year of their league's expansion from 6 to 12 teams. While I was protected in the Expansion Draft they traded me early in the season to the St. Louis Blues, once they knew Jean Ratelle was healthy and back in the line-up.

THE COLOR BLUE

Scotty Bowman, who coached Red in Hull-Ottawa, was now coaching St. Louis, which was an expansion team that year. Bowman remembered the young forward's abilities and felt he would fit into his system in St. Louis. Bowman went about acquiring both Barclay Plager and Berenson, from New York, for Ron Stewart and Ron Attwell during the 1967-68 season. While, at the time, the deal was ignored by the hockey world as just another trade, it later showed to be just one of many ingenious moves that Bowman has been credited with over his career.

The Red Baron, almost instantaneously, became an icon in St. Louis hockey, finishing the season by scoring 51 points (22-29) in 55 games and finally coming into his own as a predominate player. The following year, Red posted a career high season in points for the Blues, netting 82 (35-47) in 76 games played. His hard work help lead the Blues to three straight Stanley Cup Finals berths in 1968, 69 and 70.

On November 7, 1968, Berenson became the first modern day player to record 6 goals in a single game. The record was set at the Philadelphia Flyers expense. He continued to pay dividends for the Blues until he was dealt to the Detroit Red Wings in the 70-71 season.

Ironically, Scotty Bowman had taken over as coach in St. Louis. So, when he thought about players that he thought would help his team, he thought of me. I think the biggest reason for my success in St. Louis was that I was playing for someone who believed that I could play and expected me to play well.

I had paid my dues in the minors so obviously I was a better player when I got to St. Louis then I was when I got to Montreal. Scotty believed that I could play and he gave me every opportunity. He also knew how to play me. He played me in the role of a penalty killer and in power play situations. He put me with players that complimented me well. When you play for a coach like that you end up playing your best.

While Emile Francis was a great coach in New York, I don't think he ever believed deep down that I could play the way I thought I could play. As a player, you either play up to your coaches expectations, or you play down to them. I think in my case that was true.

I can't tell you that Scotty and I were friends when I played, we didn't have much of a personal relationship. But, he knew the game and was extremely dedicated. He expected to win every night and tried to find a way to win. He sold me on how hard you had to work and how you had to dedicate yourself both on the ice and off. He got you to raise you expectations night after night and day after day. There was even pressure in practice, and I liked that.

Scotty found players that thrived on him. They just didn't survive with him, they thrived on his style. He was hard on our team. He worked us hard and punished us. He challenged us and threatened us. There was a lot of negative motivation, but we all knew he made us play better. He would make you feel good about yourself. We ended up in the Stanley Cup finals three years in a row. A big part of that was Scotty Bowman.

BANISHED TO MOTOWN

Much like what happened to Ted Lindsay years before, Berenson was swept off to Detroit in a move to try to break the NHL Players Association. At the time Berenson had been the NHLPA's president for about three years and several recent decisions by the Union didn't sit well with the owners.[4]

The trade was difficult for me, as I really felt that my heart was in St. Louis. I was captain of the team. But, one of the things that worked against me was that I was the president of the NHL Players Association. We had had our meeting during the All-Star break and a couple of things happened that the owners were really disappointed in.

As a result, our owner asked me to resign as president. I refused, telling him that what we were doing was not wrong. We were just trying to do what was in the best interest of the game and the players and still be something that the owners could live with. I think that that had a lot to do with my leaving St. Louis.

Both Tim Eccelstone, who was our Players' Representative at the time, and myself were traded to Detroit. I think if you ask Scotty now, off the record, he would say that he didn't want to make that trade. But, at least he got a good player in return. Gary Unger was a young player then and I was older.

It was tough for me to come into Detroit. I was honored to play for the Red Wings, there was a lot of tradition there,

---

[4] In 1971, Berenson was traded to Detroit, along with Tim Eccelstone, in exchange for Gary Unger and Wayne Connelly, when he refused to abdicate his position with the NHLPA.

however, there were so many new players on the team. They had just traded (Frank) Mahovlich, (Pete) Stemkowski, and (Bruce) MacGregor. You could go right down the whole team and there were more players living in the hotel where we were staying then there were living in Detroit.

It was a real transition. It was very hard for me to come from a team that was in first place to one that was literally in last place and not winning. I was there for three and a half years and we never made the playoffs. That was very disappointing. There wasn't much to brag about.

We had a good team though. One year we had 86 points and still missed the playoffs. We drafted Marcel Dionne and he was a good player, but we just couldn't win.

BACK TO BLUE

Ironically enough, Berenson's banishment only last three and a half years as the St. Louis organization re-acquired his rights in late 1974 following an ownership change with the Blues. He remained a Bluenote past his retirement in 1978.

After 261 regular season goals and 397 assists in 986 games, Berenson made the move to the coaching ranks first as an assistant coach and then head coach of the St. Louis Blues. In 1981, as the St. Louis bench boss, Berenson earned the Jack Adams Trophy as NHL Coach of the Year.

I was obviously a different player when I went back to St. Louis. I was four years older. I was 31 when I left St. Louis and 35 when I came back. My role was a little different as a result.

They still had Unger on the team, as well as Chuck Lefly, plus several younger players. I was now one of the veterans on the team along with goaltender Eddie Johnston, Rod Seiling, Jimmy Roberts, Bob Plager and Barclay Plager. So we had a mix of veterans and young players.

At the time, St. Louis was in transition again. The stability was gone. The Solomon's had sold the team. Scotty Bowman was gone, they just brought in Emile Francis from New York, who I thought did a good job of stabilizing the franchise. But there were a lot of changes since I had left.

I survived the next four years there and actually was playing well my final year, at 38 years of age. I wanted to play another year, but Emile wanted me to retire. Barclay Plager had taken over the team as the head coach and he wanted me to stay and help him as an assistant coach.

I really had no ambition towards coaching, but I thought it would keep me in the game. I knew the team, I knew the league and I knew the game. I felt comfortable making the move, except I didn't have any coaching experience. I was an assistant coach under Barclay for one year before he took sick, and they asked me to take over the team for the rest of the season.

The following year I came back as head coach and we had a young team. Our team had a great year. Mike Liut led the team in goal and had a terrific season. He won the Lester Pearson Award (outstanding player as voted by the NHLPA members) that season and was runner up that year to Wayne Gretzky for the Hart Trophy.

Our whole team had a great year, offensively and defensively, we finished second overall in the NHL. Emile (Francis) was named the Executive of the Year and I was selected as the Coach of the Year (Jack Adams Trophy).

I made the move from player to coach, but it is difficult. It is hard to be a player's friend and then go into a coaching role where you are not always their friend. There are times, as a coach, that you are positive and supportive, but there are also times where you are not. You have to be able to do that. Plager had just done that, as well as Al Arbour, so I think I sensed how I needed to adjust.

RETURNING TO HIS ALMA MATER

It was in 1984 that Berenson decided he wanted to return to his roots, so to speak, as he accepted a position as the head coach of the University of Michigan Wolverines in the Central Collegiate Hockey Association. After being let go by the Blues in 1982, Red was an assistant coach in Buffalo under Scotty Bowman before the U-M offer came around.

Over the years Red has put together one of the NCAA's top college hockey programs leading his Wolverines to being recognized as the winningest college team of the 1990's, capturing two NCAA Championships[5], four CCHA Championships[6] and nine consecutive NCAA Playoff appearance[7] (1991-1999).

After I lost my job in St. Louis, Scotty Bowman, who was now coaching the Buffalo Sabres, hired me as an assistant coach. I had worked with Scotty for two years and I liked Buffalo and what I was doing there, plus I still had another year on my contract.

At the time, my son Gordie was a senior in high school and was looking into colleges to attend. One day I took him to Ann Arbor, to look at the University of Michigan. While I was there, Don Canham talked to me about returning and taking over the hockey program. This was the third time this had been brought up to me during my career. The first time was when I was playing for Detroit, the second time was when I was coaching for St. Louis. This time when they approached me with it, it was something that I had to listen to.

I really had been out of touch with college hockey since Al Renfrew had retired as a coach. So I wasn't current on how Michigan had been doing, where their players were coming from or the changes in the recruiting rules. But I decided that this would be a good challenge. I certainly didn't comeback for the money, as I was making twice as much money coaching in Buffalo as what I made at Michigan.

I like the people here, and I believe in players getting a college education, as I had done. I really like Michigan. I have a lot of friends here. We have a great faculty and staff in both the athletic and academic departments. Some of my former teachers were still teaching here when I came back.

---

[5] Michigan won NCAA Championships in 1996 & 1998.
[6] Michigan won CCHA Championships in 1994, 1996, 1997 & 1999.
[7] Michigan appeared in the NCAA Playoffs in each year from 1991-1999.

They just got me at the right time and I made the decision to return.

The very successful hockey program iced by the University of Michigan in the last 16 years of the 20th century, was the result of Berenson's hard work and knowledge of the game. By building one step at a time and always looking towards the future, Red was able to assemble college hockey's best team of the 1990s.

It is a big investment. I made not only an investment in my career, but a personal investment in terms of time. It's not just two or three years. When I came here, I didn't come looking for a NHL job, because there were plenty of those positions open at the time that I could have been a viable candidate for.

I had my mind set on changing the image of Michigan hockey once I found out what that image was and that I didn't like it. I wanted it to be the way I thought it should be – to be considered one of the best programs in the country. It wasn't good enough to be the best in our area or our league.

When people talk about the best college hockey programs, I wanted Michigan to be one of those names. I wanted the program to have consistency over time, not just a once in a while championship. Michigan is usually a team that is going to be there, and after a while it becomes a team that people talk about as a dynasty. Not just a dynasty that Red Berenson built, but a one in which a lot of great players played in and graduated from.

There is a loyalty and a tradition in Michigan hockey that I sensed when I was playing in Montreal. I wanted it to be a team that played like the old Montreal Canadiens, too. They'd play both ends of the ice and forecheck. They didn't play the trap, they didn't hang on, and they were a team that really tried to beat you every minute. That's how we've been, and we took our lumps doing so.

The first few years we weren't good enough to successfully play that style and we took our lumps and lost. I also had a lot to learn about college hockey, coaching, recruiting and academic issues.

We play a wide-open, hard-hitting, hard-skating game. We want to be the fastest, most skilled team in college hockey. I can't say we did that every year, but we have had our moments.

Berenson has graduated a number of his players to the National Hockey League over his years at Michigan. Among these names have been Brendan Morrison, Steve Shields, Marty Turco, Jeff Norton, Mike Knuble, Chris Tamer, Aaron Ward and Billy Muckalt.

We've had a lot of good players. I think they come here for the right reasons and we have graduated most of our players. We are not just bringing kids in to be pro hockey players, we are bringing them in to have a great experience at Michigan, because we all know that you may, or may not, play much after college hockey.

The first great defenseman that we had was probably Jeff Norton. Jeff was a freshman the year I got to Michigan. He played three years for us and was our best defenseman each year. He went to the U.S. Olympic team and played there before signing with the Islanders.

Denny Felsner was one that had a great career at Michigan and was never really successful at the NHL level. We all felt he had the tools, but it just shows you that it doesn't happen just because you are a great college player. There is a lot of learning to do when you leave here.

I had kids like Brendan Morrison that you just knew were going to be great players, but he was a good student and person as well. Those are the types of kids that you want to bring in. He led the country in scoring when he was here, won the Hobey Baker Award and just brought something special to the Michigan program.

We also had great players that didn't get attention like Morrison. David Harlock was a great player here for four years, and was a three-year captain. He was a top student but didn't make the NHL for about four or five years.

Mike Knuble and Aaron Ward were two of the first players that I coached here that won a Stanley Cup. Since they played in the area for the Detroit Red Wings, they received a lot more visibility.

The thing I like about most of our players that have moved on, is that they still call and stop in. Some come back and spend their summers here. They still feel like they are part of the family.

At age 60, Red does not see himself going anywhere else in the near future. His plans are to leave the bench as head coach of Michigan, with his team at the top of their game.

I would like to retire from this job. This will probably be my last job in terms of a full time coaching position. I don't know that I will do anything after I leave coaching, I really like what I have been doing. I like the kids, but I think there will be a time that I need to step aside and let someone else take over.

I'd like this program to be in great shape. We are currently trying to endow all of our scholarships. That is one of my goals. I hope we can do that in the next few years, so that the interest off the scholarships will literally pay for the scholarships, which is a big part of our financial nut that we are trying to crack.

Our program is making money, and that was one of my goals when I came here. I wanted to change the image of the program and make it financially profitable.

I have had a lot of help. This has not been a one-man show, it has been a team effort. I have had great support from our Athletic Department. Hockey wasn't a big thing when I came back, it was actually on the decline. It just wasn't what it is now, and a lot of people have helped in terms of marketing, ticketing, our athletic directors and academic support. Plus the reputation of Michigan does a lot in helping us recruit top players.

I have had a great staff over the years. I have only had a handful of assistant coaches and they have all been very loyal. I have a secretary, De Aronson, that has been the glue in our office and she has been here for 14 of my 15 years. In addition, we have a loyal equipment manager in Ian Hume who contributes to the stability and success of this program.

It has been rewarding to have worked with so many good people as well as good players.

RED BERENSON'S CAREER STATS

Season	Team	League	GP	G	A	Pts	PIM
1961-62	Montreal Canadiens	NHL	4	1	2	3	4
1962-63	Hull-Ottawa Canadiens	EPHL	30	23	25	48	28
1962-63	Montreal Canadiens	NHL	37	2	6	8	15
1963-64	Montreal Canadiens	NHL	69	7	9	16	12
1964-65	Quebec Aces	AHL	65	22	34	56	16
1964-65	Montreal Canadiens	NHL	3	1	2	3	0
1965-66	Quebec Aces	AHL	34	17	36	53	14
1965-66	Montreal Canadiens	NHL	23	3	4	7	12
1966-67	New York Rangers	NHL	30	0	5	5	2
1967-68	New York Rangers	NHL	19	2	1	3	2
1967-68	St. Louis Blues	NHL	55	22	29	51	22
1968-69	St. Louis Blues	NHL	76	35	47	82	43
1969-70	St. Louis Blues	NHL	67	33	39	72	38
1970-71	St. Louis Blues	NHL	45	16	26	42	12
1970-71	Detroit Red Wings	NHL	24	5	12	17	4

RED BERENSON'S CAREER STATS (CONT.)

Season	Team	League	GP	G	A	Pts	PIM
1971-72	Detroit Red Wings	NHL	78	28	41	69	16
1972-73	Detroit Red Wings	NHL	78	13	30	43	8
1973-74	Detroit Red Wings	NHL	76	24	42	66	28
1974-75	Detroit Red Wings	NHL	27	3	3	6	8
1974-75	St. Louis Blues	NHL	44	12	19	31	12
1975-76	St. Louis Blues	NHL	72	20	27	47	9
1976-77	St. Louis Blues	NHL	80	21	28	49	8
1977-78	St. Louis Blues	NHL	80	13	25	38	12
	NHL Totals		987	261	397	658	267

RED BERENSON'S COACHING RECORD

Season	Team	League	G	W	L	T	Pct.
1979-80	St. Louis Blues	NHL	56	27	20	9	.563
1980-81	St. Louis Blues	NHL	80	45	18	17	.669
1981-82	St. Louis Blues	NHL	68	28	34	6	.456
	NHL Total		204	100	72	32	.559

RED BERENSON'S COACHING RECORD (CONT.)

Season	Team	League	G	W	L	T	Pct.
1984-85	Michigan Wolverines	CCHA	40	13	26	1	.338
1985-86	Michigan Wolverines	CCHA	38	12	26	0	.316
1986-87	Michigan Wolverines	CCHA	40	14	25	1	.363
1987-88	Michigan Wolverines	CCHA	41	22	19	0	.537
1988-89	Michigan Wolverines	CCHA	41	22	15	4	.595
1989-90	Michigan Wolverines	CCHA	42	24	12	6	.643
1990-91	Michigan Wolverines	CCHA	47	34	10	3	.772
1991-92	Michigan Wolverines	CCHA	44	32	9	3	.780
1992-93	Michigan Wolverines	CCHA	40	30	7	3	.788
1993-94	Michigan Wolverines	CCHA	41	33	7	1	.817
1994-95	Michigan Wolverines	CCHA	39	30	8	1	.782
1995-96	Michigan Wolverines	CCHA	43	34	7	2	.814
1996-97	Michigan Wolverines	CCHA	43	35	4	4	.860
1997-98	Michigan Wolverines	CCHA	46	34	11	1	.750
1998-99	Michigan Wolverines	CCHA	42	25	11	6	.666
	NCAA Total		**627**	**394**	**197**	**36**	**.657**

Robert Dirk

NHL Career: 1987-1996 (9 seasons)
NHL Teams: St. Louis Blues, Vancouver, Chicago Blackhawks, Anaheim Mighty Ducks, Montreal Canadiens

Robert Dirk was never known for his offensive punch, scoring just 13 goals and 29 assists in 402 NHL matches, adding one assist in 39 playoff games. The 6'4" 215-pound defenseman was more at home playing a positional game in which he was able to use his size to slow down his opponents and protect in front of his net. This is the job he did best, gathering 786 penalty minutes over his regular season career.

Originally drafted by St. Louis, while playing junior hockey for the Western Hockey League's Regina Pats, Dirk played parts of four seasons with the Blues before being traded to Vancouver in 1991. After 217 games over three years in Vancouver, he finished the 1993-94 season playing 6 games for the Chicago Blackhawks. Dirk played nearly the next two seasons with the Mighty Ducks of Anaheim closing his career with Montreal following the All-Star break in the 1995-96 season.

Following his NHL career, Dirk split his time between the International Hockey League's Detroit Vipers and Chicago Wolves in the 1996-97 season, before retiring as a player to start a career in coaching.

A YOUTH IN WESTERN CANADA

Born in Regina, Saskatchewan on August 20, 1966, Dirk spent a good portion of his young life in British Columbia's interior. His junior hockey days were spent in his birth-town playing for the Regina Pats of the Western Hockey League.

I was born in Saskatchewan, but grew up in British Columbia. Like every Canadian boy, I had the dream to someday play in the National Hockey League. U.S. boys want to play baseball, football or basketball but, back when I was a kid, it was every Canadian boy's dream to play in the NHL. I was fortunate enough to have it come true. That's what I geared my whole life towards.

My parents tell me that I started skating when I was about 2 years old. They said I would sit in front of the TV every Saturday night with my hockey gloves on, and holding my stick, while I watched Hockey Night in Canada. I would sit there and watch the whole game. I don't remember that, but that is what they tell me.

I played my minor hockey growing up in Kelowna, British Columbia. I definitely wasn't one of the best players when I played. I was always bigger and stronger, but with that came the coordination factor. I was gangly and off balance, but that was probably good for me, as I always had to work that much harder to make sure I made the team and to step up to the next level. I think that eventually helped me in getting to the NHL.

I was never, ever, the best player on my team. I was one of those guys that always had to work hard and do the little things to contribute to the hockey club. That is the attitude I took into the NHL.

It's funny. People always talk about the politics in hockey and it is true. Even in minor hockey I can remember coaches being picked because they were friends with somebody on the committee. Because they were picked, their children would make the team. Not necessarily because they deserved to, but because of who they knew.

At 15, my parents decided that if I was to give this a good shot (turning professional), I had to go away. So I left home and moved about 1,000 miles away to a boarding school. I went out to Saskatchewan to the Notre Dame Hounds and played there for a year. That really helped. In minor hockey we practiced once or twice a week and played one or two games on weekends. At Notre Dame we were on the ice every single day. Getting on the ice everyday was a big stepping stone for my career.

There was a lot of competition. Kids were coming from across all of Canada to play on our midget teams. It was an enlightening experience. I didn't make the triple-A team, I only made the double-A team, but it showed me I had a future if I kept working hard. It also showed me I had a long way to go.

Then at 16, my junior career started. I started that season with the Regina Pats and remained there until I turned professional at 19.

Junior hockey was great. I believe it's for the NHL to get to see the young players more in the NHL light. They are playing 72 games a season, unlike the Universities in the States or Canada where they only play 2 games on the weekend. In juniors they are playing more thus they get more adapted to the professional life with the traveling, the bus rides, and basically being on your own.

Contrary to that, players come out of the universities at 21 or 22 years old with more maturity. They are better prepared to make that first step compared to those coming out of junior.

I loved junior. It was a lot of fun. You still have the dream that you are going to make it to the NHL, and you are away from home for the first time. You are sowing your wild oats. It's part of growing up. I made a lot of friendships there, guys that I played with for three or four years. It was a lot of fun, but it wasn't easy. A lot of kids can't leave home when they are 15 or 16-years-old. It forces you to grow up real fast.

BEING DRAFTED AND GOING PRO

The St. Louis Blues selected Dirk with their 4th choice (53rd overall) in the 1984 NHL Entry Draft. He spent his first year out of juniors (1986-87) playing with the Blues' International Hockey League farm-club in Peoria. For his next four seasons, he would split his time between the Peoria Rivermen and the parent club.

The year that Dirk was drafted yielded a bumper crop of NHL talent. First round selections that draft included Mario Lemieux, Kirk Muller, Ed Olczyk, Al Iafrate, Petr Svoboda, Shawn

Burr, Shayne Corson, Sylvain Cote and Gary Roberts to name a few.

I didn't expect St. Louis to draft me. In the previous fall (1983), St. Louis was in Regina for their training camp. They saw me there first and remembered me, following me through the season. However, I thought I was going to end up going to either Washington or Chicago.

I was in Montreal for the draft and it was exciting to be sitting in the stands, waiting for my name to be called out. I heard 52 names called before mine. Every time another name was called besides my own, it was like a knife being stuck in me. You start thinking that you are never going to be picked. Then once you hear your name, it's like a dream come true. It is like being on death row until you are called, then it's like a big weight being lifted off your shoulders. But it's only your first step.

I was rated to go anywhere between the second to the fourth round. It was quite a draft that year. Mario Lemieux went first and Kirk Muller went second. There were a lot of guys from that draft that are still playing today and went on to have superstar careers. Maybe I was born in the wrong year.

After I was drafted, I went to the fall training camps for two years, but was always returned to my junior team. I wasn't physically, or mentally, ready. It is very hard to step right into the NHL at 18 or 19 years of age. I really wasn't prepared, but junior hockey is a great breading ground for player development.

Even when I signed my first professional contract at 20, I wasn't ready for the NHL. It took me almost another three years to learn the craft. Playing defense is probably the hardest position there is out there. It's a learning experience.

It gets frustrating those first couple of years, at 21 and 22, because you think you are good enough. You don't want to be in the minors, you want to be in the big times. Looking back at it now, I know I wasn't ready. They say, as you grow older you grow smarter. That is true. There is no way I was ready back then.

By the time I was 24-years-old, I had learn the position and learned what I could and couldn't do. You learn what your strengths are and what your weaknesses are. That is part of growing up and becoming a professional hockey player. Once I was able to make the transition, and I knew I could play, it was just a matter of going out, being consistent and doing it night after night.

Dirk was never disillusioned about his abilities. He knew that in order to contribute to his team, he would need to play a very hard-hitting defensive role - one in which he used his size to punish his opponents rather than out-maneuver them. While Dirk was a tough player, he was also a relatively clean player who used his position on the ice to slow his opposition down.

I was 6'4" and played at 215-pounds, so I definitely had to use my size to my advantage. But, when push came to shove, I had to be there for my teammates.

Once I got up to St. Louis, I had to learn how to play at the NHL level. Everything is a step fast there. Things happen quickly. It's a process you have to learn. You have to earn it and it took me a while. But once I got there, I was there for a while.

VANCOUVER CANUCKS

Dirk's best season with the Blues was in 1990-91, when he played 41 games before being traded to the Vancouver Canucks.[8] While with the Canucks, Dirk would play in 217 games and score 9 of his 13 career goals. He also accumulated 401 of his 786 total penalty minutes in Vancouver.

Sadly for Dirk, the Canucks would deal him to the Chicago Blackhawks at the trade deadline of the 1993-94 season to make room on the roster for newly acquired Brian Glynn. That season

---

[8] Dirk was included in a deal that also sent Geoff Courtnall, Cliff Ronning and Sergio Momesso to Vancouver in exchange for Dan Quinn and Garth Butcher.

saw the Canucks make a Cinderella playoff run going all the way to the Stanley Cup finals before being dropped by the New York Rangers in seven games.

I am the type of person that is very loyal and giving to people that give it back to me. The way I look at the trade was that I was with the St. Louis organization for eight years and I never wanted to go anywhere else. I always wanted to play in St. Louis. They drafted me and gave me the opportunity to play in the NHL, so when I was traded, it was tough. It was real tough.

On the one hand it was like they were saying, 'We don't want you.' That's a tough thing to deal with. On the other hand, somebody did want me. It turned out that getting traded from St. Louis to Vancouver was the best career move for me. The only negative was the timing.

At the time, St. Louis was battling Chicago for first place in the Norris Division and the league's top spot overall. We had just over taken them and were up by about 3-5 points. Then right at the deadline, they traded four of us away.

Needless to say, Chicago overtook them and St. Louis was bounced in the first round. We (St. Louis) felt that we had a legitimate shot at the Stanley Cup that year, and for that to be taken away was tough. But on the other hand, I went to Vancouver and they were the best three years of my career. You lose something, but you also gain something.

Since I grew up in Kelowna, British Columbia, which is four hours east of Vancouver, going to Vancouver was basically playing in my hometown. That was a lot of fun. I always had family, or friends, coming in to see me play. It's something special to play in your hometown, especially in the NHL.

Vancouver was a very close knit team. All the guys there were outcasts and driftwood from other organizations. Pat Quinn assembled us and we went from last to first, all the way to the Stanley Cup finals. It was a growing experience for all of us.

What made it special was that we were 20 guys that nobody wanted, and we turned out to be a pretty good hockey club. It was an unselfish hockey club. We really had no superstars at the time. We were all pretty young, and we realized that if the team did well, we'd all do well. As a result, guys were doing the little things that make a difference – blocking shots, and sticking up for each other. Fortunately, we got a kid by the name of Pavel Bure, who came in and scored the key goals at the right time.

It was a great situation that was led by a great man. Pat Quinn is one of the smartest hockey men I have ever come across. I felt that I learned the most from him. He was an ex-NHL defenseman. He was 6'4", 210-pounds, the same as me. He taught me a lot. I credit him for much of my success.

DUCK SOUP

Following his trade to Chicago, where he only played 6 games, Dirk started the 1994-95 season with the Mighty Ducks of Anaheim, who were in their second season of existence. Playing in 82 games over a season and a half with the Ducks, Dirk managed 2 goals, 5 assists and 82 penalty minutes before being dealt to Montreal.[9]

I was in my fourth year with the Canucks when I was traded to Chicago. Vancouver was struggling as a team and needed a boost. They made a big trade with St. Louis and picked up two defensemen in the deal – Jeff Brown and Bret Hedican. Since we already had seven defensemen before the trade, somebody had to go.

From what I understand, they tried to unload some other players before me, but my contract, being what it was, made it easier to move me. I went to Chicago and once again it was a case of losing something and gaining something.

It was the last year that the Blackhawks would play in old Chicago Stadium, so I was able to play in the last game there. That was really something special. It was always my favorite place to play as an opposing player. I loved playing in the stadium with the fans right there. Then, after the trade, it was even more exciting to hear the fans going nuts during the anthem

---

[9] Dirk was traded to the Canadiens in exchange for right wing Jim Campbell.

and knowing it was for you. You had goose bumps all the time. I can always tell my grandchildren that I played the last game in Chicago Stadium.

Unfortunately, we lost to Toronto in the first round of the playoffs while Vancouver made it to the Stanley Cup Finals. That was the year that Wendell (Clark), (Doug) Gilmour and the boys lit it up and took the Leafs to the Western Conference Finals. They beat us out in six games. We had some injuries, but there were also some internal problems at the time. Things just weren't going well in Chicago, and the team has been in a downward spiral ever since.

The next season, I signed as a free agent with the Anaheim Mighty Ducks, and was reunited with Ron Wilson, who had been an assistant coach when I was in Vancouver. Wilson was the Ducks head coach at the time.

I was looking for a place where I could play and get along with the coach, and had always gotten along really well with Ronnie in Vancouver. He would stay around and help me after practices, so we had a good rapport. Being as I was an older guy coming to a young hockey club, he made me an assistant captain. That was good experience.

Anaheim was great. So was living in California. I think, at the time, we were playing in the nicest facility in the NHL, The Pond. We had some tough years there until we got (Paul) Kariya and (Teemu) Selanne. You are always trying for the Stanley Cup but, unfortunately, we knew we weren't going to get it being a second-year franchise. But it was a chance to play in the NHL, you can't ask for anything more than that.

Playing hockey in California was very different. Guys would bring their golf clubs and surfboards in their cars when they came to practice. Afterwards they would go to the beach or the course. It was a different mentality, for sure. If you are winning and things are going well, then that's great. But it was tough sometimes because it seemed like some guys were more interested in living the life in California then they were in doing their job. Winning games and getting the two points is what pays the bills.

When you play in other hockey towns like Vancouver, St. Louis and Chicago you are pretty much in a fishbowl. When you go out everyone recognizes you. But in Anaheim you could go anywhere you wanted and nobody knew who you were. That part was nice. It is nice to get away sometimes. To be able to go out and be with yourself or your friends and family. The other sports teams out there – the Lakers, Dodgers and Angels – they are in the fishbowl compared to the hockey players.

A CAREER ENDING BREAK

Dirk played about two and a half seasons with the Ducks before being traded to Montreal. In his first game with Les Habs, Dirk suffered a career-ending shoulder injury while playing against the Tampa Bay Lightning. The injury sidelined Dirk and, for all intents and purposes, ended his career.

Dirk played the following season in the IHL, starting with the Detroit Vipers before being traded to the Chicago Wolves midway through the year. Once again fate slapped the veteran defenseman's face, as the Vipers raced all the way to the Turner Cup Championship.

It was right at the All-Star break and Montreal was looking to shore up their defense, and at that time Anaheim was looking to get younger and build for the future. So, at first, it appeared to be a good trade for both sides.

I got to Montreal, after taking the red-eye all night, and basically broke my shoulder 10-minutes into my first game with them. That had a lot to do with my NHL career ending the way it did. It was the first game after the All-Star break and I was on my third shift in the first period against Tampa Bay when I was hit. The kid that hit me had just been called up to play in his first and only NHL game. He never played in the NHL after that night. I can't even recall his name. I was three feet from the boards, in that no-man zone, was off-balance a bit, got hit, went into the boards and broke my shoulder in two spots.

When it happened, I knew it was broken. I went to the hospital and the doctors said I needed to be out six full weeks in order to allow it to recuperate and heal. Four weeks in my rehab, we were struggling as a team and Montreal's head coach, Mario Tremblay, came to me and said he wanted me to play. The attitude I always had was if the coach wants you to play, you go out and play.

I wasn't healthy or ready to return. I should have taken the full six weeks and I didn't. That was basically the end of my career. It was really a disheartening situation. Basically, Mario Tremblay and myself mix like oil and water. For whatever reason, he didn't take too kindly to me, and I didn't take too kindly to him.

At that point it was agreed upon that the best thing for me to do was to go home and get healed. So that's what I did.

They say things happen for a reason. The way I look at it, my NHL career ended on a wrong note, but because of it ending, I signed with the Detroit Vipers of the International Hockey League. I got to know them very well and they took a liking to me. They saw that maybe I could become a coach someday. Because of them, I'm doing what I am doing today.

Playing in the IHL was a different role. The previous two years, playing in the NHL wasn't fun anymore. I always told myself that when it got to the point where I wasn't having fun playing anymore, it was time to get out of the game. I wasn't going to stick around and play just for the money.

At the time, early in the season in Detroit, Brad Shaw, who was their player/assistant coach, had immigration problems. So, Steve Ludzik (Detroit head coach) and Rick Dudley (Vipers' GM) asked me to fill that role. That was how I got into coaching. All of a sudden, playing was fun again.

That team was probably the closest bunch of guys of any team I ever played on. They went on to win the Turner Cup that season. No matter whom you walked out the door with after practice, you could have lunch with them and enjoy each other's company. I credit that to Dudley and Ludzik. It's not always the best talented team that wins championships. Character on the ice and in the dressing room, as well as togetherness, can also win it for you.

Nearly missing championships was the story of my career. As a 16-year-old I was playing midget hockey in Regina, for the Pat-Canadiens, when I was called up to play junior for the rest of the year. That midget team I left behind, went on to win the Air Canada Cup (Canadian national championship). Then, when I was in my fourth year pro in Peoria, I was called up to St. Louis in January for the rest of the year and Peoria went on to win the Turner Cup. In 1994, I was traded from Vancouver to Chicago and the Canucks went on to nearly win the Stanley Cup, losing in seven games to the Rangers. Then I get to the Detroit Vipers, get traded to the Chicago Wolves in January 1997, and Detroit goes on to win the Turner Cup. Then the Wolves win it the next year after I retired. I guess, as a player, it just wasn't meant to be. Missing all those championships as a player, is just going to make it even sweeter when I win one as a coach. I don't know when it'll happen, but it'll happen.

BEHIND THE BENCH

Following his playing career, Dirk instantly traded his lumber and sweater for a clipboard and wool suits, as he made the move behind the bench. In his first season a head coach with the United Hockey League's Winston-Salem (NC) IceHawks, Dirk received Coach of the Year honors for his efforts.

The next season saw Dirk move to Saginaw, Michigan where he took over the reigns of the newly renamed Gears in the UHL. Midway through the season, Gears ownership decided to forsake a team that was becoming costly to run, putting all of their efforts into their other team in nearby Flint.

Eventually Dirk's team was dwindled down to a little over two-handful of players as only 11 players were suited up for their remaining month of play. It was a worse case nightmare for any hockey coach, especially considering several of the players were picked up from local men's leagues.

As a player I always thought about becoming a coach. They (Dudley and Ludzik) made some calls and gave me the opportunity to get into coaching. The way my career was going at the time, it was the best thing for me. I knew my days were numbered as a player. This way I can be in the game for possibly another 30 years.

Rick Dudley basically got me the opportunity down in Winston-Salem to coach for the 1997-98 season. Making the move from player to coach isn't that difficulty. Hockey is hockey. It's just a matter of getting the respect of the players, getting them to trust you and trust in your systems. We didn't have the most talented team, but the guys came in, worked hard and gave a 100 percent effort. Fortunately for myself, people recognized that and I was awarded Coach of the Year my first year. It was sort of unbelievable, considering we had a losing record.

I was coerced to coming to Saginaw the next year, and was told a story that never transpired. I was told that time, effort and money was being put into the franchise and it was going to get turned around. Needless to say, that was far from the truth.

But, I still enjoy coaching. From what has happened the last two years, I wouldn't trade it for the world. I also wouldn't wish it on my worse enemy. I have learned a lot from it and it has only made me a better person and a better coach.

I had probably the worst year ever in hockey by a coach, and I made it through. The biggest thing in coming back to Saginaw for the second year is that we have new ownership. They know what they have to do. They know they have to spend money to get quality players. But my biggest thing is that I have some scores to settle within the league and there is no better place for me to do it than in Saginaw.

To go from worst to first would look good on my coaching resume. I am just like the players at this level; I am in the same boat looking to move up. To do that I have to win.

At the end of the 98-99 season I only had 11 players dressed for every game, and half those players shouldn't have been playing in the league. They weren't even qualified. All that was left was the 11 players, Jason Wood (trainer) and myself.

We struggled the last four weeks of the season with bodies. I'd be lying if I said we didn't think about quitting. We all did, but we had come that far and didn't want to quit on each other. We made it though the season.

Dirk remains as much a competitor behind the bench as he was on the ice. While he has experienced both ends of the coaching spectrum, he is still young and hopes to enjoy a long, successful coaching career before he calls it quits.

The dream is to eventually to get to the NHL as a coach. I was there as a player and I want to get back to it as a coach. As I said before, hockey is hockey. I believe that I can teach the game. I have learned what to do from some great people, and what not to do from some very bad people. Now, it's just a matter of getting into the right situation at the right time.

The ball is in my court, and I have to do it right. Coaching is just like when you are a player, you have to win to move up, and that is what I plan on doing. If it doesn't come true, then I will remain coaching at the UHL or AHL level the rest of my career. That is okay too. At least I'm doing something that I love.

ROBERT DIRK'S CAREER STATS

Season	Team	League	GP	G	A	Pts	PIM
1982-83	Regina Pats	WHL	1	0	0	0	0
1983-84	Regina Pats	WHL	62	2	10	12	64
1984-85	Regina Pats	WHL	69	10	34	44	97
1985-86	Regina Pats	WHL	72	19	60	79	140
1986-87	Peoria Rivermen	IHL	76	5	17	22	155
1987-88	Peoria Rivermen	IHL	54	4	21	25	126
1987-88	St. Louis Blues	NHL	7	0	1	1	16
1988-89	Peoria Rivermen	IHL	22	0	2	2	54
1988-89	St. Louis Blues	NHL	9	0	1	1	11
1989-90	Peoria Rivermen	IHL	24	1	2	3	79
1989-90	St. Louis Blues	NHL	37	1	1	2	128
1990-91	Peoria Rivermen	IHL	3	0	0	0	2
1990-91	St. Louis Blues	NHL	41	1	3	4	100
1990-91	Vancouver Canucks	NHL	11	1	0	1	20
1991-92	Vancouver Canucks	NHL	72	2	7	9	126

ROBERT DIRK'S CAREER STATS
(Cont.)

Season	Team	League	GP	G	A	Pts	PIM
1992-93	Vancouver Canucks	NHL	69	4	8	12	150
1993-94	Vancouver Canucks	NHL	65	2	3	5	105
1993-94	Chicago Blackhawks	NHL	6	0	0	0	26
1994-95	Anaheim Mighty Ducks	NHL	38	1	3	4	56
1995-96	Anaheim Mighty Ducks	NHL	44	1	2	3	42
1995-96	Montreal Canadiens	NHL	3	0	0	0	6
1996-97	Detroit Vipers	IHL	48	2	8	10	36
1996-97	Chicago Wolves	IHL	31	1	5	6	26
	NHL Totals		**402**	**13**	**29**	**42**	**786**

Bill Gadsby

NHL Career: 1946-66 (20 seasons)
NHL Teams: Chicago Blackhawks, New York Rangers, Detroit Red Wings
Hockey Hall of Fame Induction: 1970

Bill Gadsby broke into the NHL with the Chicago Blackhawks during the 1946-47 season. During his 19 NHL seasons, Gadsby was named First Team All-Star three times[10], Second Team All-Star four times[11], and was known for playing both an offensive and defensive style of defense.

Gadsby stayed in Chicago until the day before Thanksgiving in 1954 when he, along with Pete Conacher, were traded to the New York Rangers for Al Stanley and Nick Mickoski.

Gadsby, who was known to be a gutsy defenseman with the Blackhawks, carried that style to New York where, in his first game with the Broadway Blues, Gadsby dove in front of a Boston Bruins shot, preventing a goal but breaking several bones in the process.

Gadsby remained with the Rangers until the 1961-62 season when Muzz Patrick dealt him to Detroit, for Les Hunt and cash, where he remained for five seasons before retiring in 1966.

GROWING UP

Bill Gadsby was born and raised in Calgary, Alberta where he began his hockey days, at the age of five, playing on the frozen ponds and the streets.

---

[10] Gadsby was named as a First Team All-Star in 1956, 1958 and 1959.
[11] Gadsby was named a Second Team All-Star in 1953, 1954, 1957 and 1965.

There was only one indoor rink in Calgary at that time," says Gadsby. "I played in the communities outdoor rinks. I didn't play organized hockey until I was about 13. At fourteen, I played in juvenile hockey. I had a tryout for a team and didn't make it, but there was a fellow there who took all the rejects. He formed his own team and we won the Alberta championship for the Juvenile league.

There was no junior "A" in Calgary at that time, but Edmonton had a team and they wanted me to go there. So, I went to Edmonton, when I was sixteen, played two years of junior there, finished my high school and turned pro with Chicago when I was 18.

It was during these days in junior hockey that Gadsby credits good coaching from Earl Robertson, who played goal for the New York Americans and Detroit Red Wings, as helping him on his way to The Show.

We played a lot of hockey in those two years I was there (Edmonton), practiced a lot and I had good coaching. I learned a lot from Earl Robertson when I was 16 and 17.

Then Clarence Moher, who was the Chief Western Scout for the Detroit Red Wings, became my coach. After playing pro for about 4 or 5 years, I got into the golf range business with him in Edmonton.

We had a steady junior league with four teams. It was a good league. We had Provincial playoffs to go to the Memorial Cup back then. We played East against West in those years.

We practiced quite a bit, and I learned a lot from my coaches in junior.

During his junior days, Gadsby's team made it to the Western Finals against Winnipeg by beating a Moosejaw, Saskatchewan team with players such as Emile Francis, Metro Prystai and Bert Olmstead - the same Moosejaw team that a year prior had defeated them for the same spot.

THE BLACKHAWK YEARS

Gadsby move to the big league was a relatively rapid one. While many players spent several years in a NHL team's farm system honing their skills, Gadsby was brought up to the Blackhawks after playing only 12 games with the Kansas City Pla-Mors, of the USHL, at the beginning of the 1946-47 season.

While in KC, Gadsby scored 2 goals and 3 assists before getting the call to play with the parent club. From there he never looked back.

I came up to Chicago in 1946-47, the same year Gordie (Howe) came in the league. I played in Chicago for eight years and enjoyed it. We didn't have a very good hockey club, but I played with a lot of guys that I listened to on the radio when I was growing up in Calgary. Guys like Max and Doug Bentley, (Bill) Mosienko, and Johnny Mariucci.

I played junior hockey, in western Canada, against Bert Olmstead, whom I roomed with in Chicago, and Metro Prystai and finally ended up on the same pro team as them. They were both very good hockey players.

We were playing Detroit in my first year, it was the first time I had ever played the Red Wings. Jack Stewart and Mariucci got into a fight on the ice. They went toe-to-toe before heading to the penalty box. In those days the penalty boxes were together in the same area. Once in the box, they went at it again. They were hitting each other like you wouldn't believe. At this point I'm saying to myself, 'What did I get into?' I mean, here were two guys that were tough, mean and strong. These guys went at it for maybe two or two and a half minutes, which is a long time to fight.

Another high point in Gadsby career was outscoring Gordie Howe in his first season in the NHL.

I outscored Gordie that first year. I had 8 goals and he had seven. I think he played ten more games than I did that year, too. We're still pretty good friends and I never let him forget it. After that he took off on me, though.

I was with Chicago for eight years and was traded to New York, along with Pat Conacher, for Alan Stanley and Nick Mickoski. I spent seven years in New York and had some good seasons there. I didn't like to city too well, it was a big zoo, but I was there to play hockey.

It's (New York) too big. There are too many people. Everything is cluttered all the time. We lived out on Long Island, which was good.

I had some good years there, though. I made the All-Star team five times out of seven years in New York. That part of it was good but I didn't care for the city. My wife and I enjoyed Broadway and we got to see some great shows. The nightlife was great, which we also enjoyed, but I was very happy to go to Detroit in 1961.[12]

THE DETROIT YEARS

Gadsby's joy in moving to Detroit was not only due to it allowing him to get out of New York, but also due to some talks he had with Sid Abel, who was coaching the Red Wings at the time. Sid had talked with Gadsby about becoming coach of Detroit's farm club in Edmonton after playing with the Wings for a couple of years. The idea of moving from player to coach appealed to Gadsby.

Sid had talked with me about playing in Detroit for a couple of years, then heading to Edmonton to be the coach of their farm club there. Since I lived in Edmonton, the idea appealed to me.

So they made a trade and it fell through. It (the trade) would have sent Red Kelly and Billy McNeill to go to New York for Eddie Shack and I. I was happy to be going to Detroit. It was a good club and I had heard it was a good organization, plus I

---

[12] Detroit acquired Gadsby from the Rangers in 1961 in trade for Les Hunt and cash.

wanted to get out of New York. I had had it there. The trade fell through because Red Kelly wouldn't go to New York.

The next year, I saw Sid and he said he was going to keep working on it. He said the deal would be the same, I would play two years in Detroit and head to Edmonton and maybe be a player/coach for a couple of years and then strictly coach. I said fine.

One night on the ice when I was playing for New York, Gordie Howe told me a story. He said, 'Loosen up a little bit. Your coming here tomorrow.' He was a joker anyway, so I said, 'Oh yea, let up and you guys will swamp us tonight.' Sure enough I got off the ice that night and wasn't even in the dressing room when Muzz Patrick told me he made a deal with Detroit and I was heading there tomorrow. I was really happy.

I had some good years in Detroit. We had some good hockey clubs in the 60's. We had guys like (Terry) Sawchuck, (Marcel) Pronovost, Doug Barkley, Norm Ullman, (Alex) Delvecchio, (Gordie) Howe and Parker MacDonald. We had a sound hockey club.

I must have gotten new life, or something, because I lasted in Detroit for five years. About the fourth or fifth year in Detroit, the Edmonton Flyers hockey club, Detroit's farm team, disbanded. I think they went to Fort Worth after that.

Jack Adams treated me very good in Detroit. He gave me raises every year. I think I could have played another year, but I had enough. I quit in 1966. That was the year that Montreal beat us out in the finals. Expansion was coming in 1967 and I think I could have stayed around a few more years, but I had enough. After that, I got a job coaching the Edmonton Oil Kings, a junior 'A' hockey club.

LOOKING BACK ON HIS CAREER

I have had a great life. I really enjoyed playing hockey. I even enjoyed practice that's how much I liked it. Not many guys can say that, but I think the guys that last enjoy it, otherwise they wouldn't last that long.

I played in two eras of hockey. I played against guys that were on the end of their careers.

Like in Montreal when they had Toe Blake, Elmer Lach and Maurice "Rocket" Richard with Bill Durnan in the nets and Big Emile Bouchard on defense.

Toronto had Syl Apps, Ted Kennedy and Turk Broda. I am going back to the 1946, 47, 48, 49 era.

Boston had the Kraut Line with Milt Schmidt, (Woody) Dumart and (Bobby) Bauer with Frank Brimsek in the nets.

Chicago had the Bentleys, Mosienko, and Mariucci with Emile Francis and Al Rollins in goal.

There was some pretty good hockey players from 1946-52. You only had six teams and they were all pretty deep.

Then it switched over the next ten or eleven years I played. I played against Jacques Plante, Doug Harvey and (Bernie) Geoffrion, (Yvan) Cournoyer, in Montreal. It was two different eras. It was something else.

In Boston they had (Johnny) Bucyk, (Bronco) Horvath, (Vic) Stasiuk. In Chicago it was Bobby Hull, (Stan) Mikita, Glenn Hall and (Pierre) Pilote.

It (the NHL) really went from an older situation, guys on their last legs, to a new crop coming in. So I was kind of lucky to play against a lot of good hockey players.

Over his career, Gadsby credits "Rocket" Richard, Hull and Howe as being some of the strongest players he played against.

They were big, strong and could skate well. The Rocket was very strong. He only had one thing in mind from the blue line in; he just wanted to turn that red light on.

Bobby Hull could go pretty good. He was tough to move. (Phil) Esposito was another one that was tough to move in front of the net.

(Dave) Keon, in Toronto, could really skate. Frank Mahovlich was tough to stop. He was big, strong and could really skate. He'd give you that wide berth.

Courneyor could really fly. They had some good hockey clubs in Montreal in those years. They were well balanced and had a lot of depth.

I was really luck to play against both eras.

ON ICE RIVALS, RETIRED ALUMS

While looking back on his career, Gadsby remembers several players that he developed a mutual on-ice dislike for. Players that over the years developed a mutual respect of each other, as one warrior respects another. One of those players was Stan Mikita.

I just couldn't stand Mikita at times," remarked Gadsby about their playing days. "I talked to him the other night on the phone and we're going to do a double signing on that Sports Illustrated cover from 1966. I have played golf with him for the last 15 years. We see each other at our NHL Alumni gatherings.

Gadsby remembers breaking Billy Harris' nose one night in Toronto.

I felt bad about it, but he slashed me across the ankle. I took my stick and put it right on his nose. I felt really bad about it. We see each other now and we kid about it. He says, 'Remember the night you gave me this (referring to the stick in the nose). I never played for three weeks, I couldn't see.'

Another player to fit this bill was the Rocket. Gadsby and Richard went overseas for a few old-timers games around 1976 and had some time to remember the old days.

I never knew the Rocket by playing against him. I never talked to him. He had a knack of coming down the ice and try to go wide. He'd stick out that arm and try to ward you off. So I use to take my stick and whack him about three times across his arm.

We were in Germany one night, while playing some games for the Canadian Armed Forces. While I was sitting in the Officers Quarter's bar area, having a few drinks, the Rocket came over to me. He said, "You know Bill, I have to tell you one thing. When I use to go around you, after I finished the game, the next day I was blue-black from here to here (indicating the length of his arm).'

I told him he had his arm out and he wasn't suppose to stick it out. He said, 'I didn't want to go to Detroit to play you guys.

BEATING POLIO

Gadsby's career was not all highlights though. There was a point, in 1952, where his career could have easily ended. After spending the summer of '52 back home in Edmonton, Gadsby was diagnosed with Polio. An outbreak of the debilitating disease had hit Edmonton that summer.

Polio is a disease caused by any one of three types of polio virus. Its effects range from no symptoms at all to paralysis and possible death. Symptoms include fever, tiredness, headache, nausea and vomiting, severe muscle pain and spasms, and stiffness of the neck and back, with or without weakness of one or more arms and legs. The disease is usually caught by direct contact with an infected person.

It was in the late summer, early fall of 1952 and there was a Polio epidemic in Western Canada at the time. I had just gotten married June of that year.

I had a golf driving range I owned at the time. We had about seven or eight kids working for us and five of them came down with Polio just before I went to training camp.

On my way to training camp, I was flying down from Edmonton to Toronto and I wasn't feeling too good. I threw-up a couple of times on the plane, had a very stiff neck and headaches. When I got into Toronto, I ironically met the owner of the Blackhawks, who I was playing with then. He asked me 'What the heck's wrong with you?' I said, 'I don't feel very good."

We were on our way to North Bay for training camp, which is about 140 miles north of Toronto, he told me to come with them in his limousine so I didn't have to fly.

Gadsby needed to stop the limo three times on the way up to North Bay in order to get out of the vehicle and get sick again.

Mr. Tobin, the owner of the Blackhawks, said for me to get into the hospital as soon as we got to North Bay, which I did.

They (the hospital) took some tests and some spinal fluid. From there they whipped me to Ottawa by ambulance, which is a long drive.

It turned out I had Polio and was in the hospital for about 16 or 17 days. The doctor in Ottawa said to me that I was a very luck guy. He told me that I had 48 cells in my spinal fluid and 51 would have meant paralysis.

After I got out, I went to training camp. I had two or three practices and starting playing. I was so damn happy that I got over it that I made the second All-Star team that year. About two months after that I found out my wife was pregnant.

Two of the five kids from the driving range that contracted Polio that year were paralyzed. I have seen them over the years, and they are not doing well. They can't walk and are in wheel chairs. The other three of them came out of it pretty good, though.

AFTER THE APPLAUSE

Bill Gadsby, who turned 72 in August of 1999, continues to make his home in suburban Detroit, Michigan with his wife of 47 years, Edna.

The Gadsby's have four daughters, 8 grandsons and 1 granddaughter.

Gadsby remains a member of the Red Wing Alumni even though a hip replacement a few years back put a stop to his playing in the numerous charity games that the Detroit Alum's play each year.

Gadsby continues to run the Bill Gadsby Hockey Schools where he helps teach and develop men and women in improving their game.

BILL GADSBY'S CAREER STATS

Season	Team	League	GP	G	A	Pts	PIM
1946-47	Kansas City	USHL	12	2	3	5	8
1946-47	Chicago Blackhawks	NHL	48	8	10	18	31
1947-48	Chicago Blackhawks	NHL	60	6	10	16	66
1948-49	Chicago Blackhawks	NHL	50	3	10	13	85
1949-40	Chicago Blackhawks	NHL	70	10	25	35	138
1950-51	Chicago Blackhawks	NHL	25	3	7	10	32
1952-53	Chicago Blackhawks	NHL	68	2	20	22	84
1953-54	Chicago Blackhawks	NHL	70	12	29	41	108
1954-55	Chicago Blackhawks	NHL	18	3	5	8	17
1954-55	New York Rangers	NHL	52	8	8	16	44
1955-56	New York Rangers	NHL	70	12	29	41	108
1956-57	New York Rangers	NHL	70	4	37	41	72
1957-58	New York Rangers	NHL	65	14	32	46	48
1958-59	New York Rangers	NHL	70	5	46	51	56
1959-60	New York Rangers	NHL	65	9	22	31	60

BILL GADSBY'S CAREER STATS
(Cont.)

Season	Team	League	GP	G	A	Pts	PIM
1960-61	New York Rangers	NHL	65	9	26	35	49
1961-62	Detroit Red Wings	NHL	70	7	30	37	88
1962-63	Detroit Red Wings	NHL	70	4	24	28	116
1963-64	Detroit Red Wings	NHL	64	2	16	18	80
1964-65	Detroit Red Wings	NHL	61	0	12	12	122
1965-66	Detroit Red Wings	NHL	58	5	12	17	72
NHL Totals			**1248**	**260**	**406**	**666**	**1539**

BILL GADSBY'S NHL COACHING RECORD

Season	Team	League	G	W	L	T	%
1968-69	Detroit Red Wings	NHL	78	35	31	12	.526

Dennis Hextall

NHL Career: 1968-1980 (13 Seasons)
NHL Teams: New York Rangers, Los Angeles Kings, California Golden Seals, Minnesota North Stars, Detroit Red Wings, Washington Capitals

Dennis Hextall was a second generation NHLer along with his brother Bryan Jr. Their dad, Bryan Sr., played 12 seasons for the New York Rangers and scored the Stanley Cup winning goal in 1940 against the Toronto Maple Leafs. Stretching the lineage into a third generation is Dennis' nephew Ron Hextall of the Philadelphia Flyers.

Dennis is a veteran of 13 NHL seasons (1968-1980) playing for the New York Rangers, L.A. Kings, California Golden Seals, Minnesota North Stars, Detroit Red Wings and Washington Capitals. During his career Dennis played in 681 games scoring 153 goals, 350 assists and amassing 1398 penalty minutes.

HIS EARLY DAYS

I came from a hockey family. My father's in the Hall of Fame. He played with the New York Rangers 12 years. When they won the Stanley Cup (1940), he scored the winning goal in the seventh game in overtime against Turk Broda.

My brother and I both played pro. I played in the NHL for 12 years, and Bryan played eight. However, Bryan played more minor league than I did. Now, his son (Ron) is in Philadelphia.

I think we are one of only two families that played three generations in the NHL. The only other family to qualify is the Patricks. Lester Patrick, who was the general manager of New York for years, played one or two games in the NHL. Then his sons, Lynn and Muzz, played with the Rangers. Then Lynn's son, Craig Patrick played in the NHL and is now general manager of Pittsburgh.

Hextall grew up in the Province of Manitoba playing the game he inherited from his father.[13] After advancing through the youth leagues, he started his road to the NHL by playing a couple of years of junior hockey for the Brandon Wheat Kings. In his final year in Brandon things finally fell into place for Hextall and he was offered scholarships to four different U.S. colleges.

I'm from Manitoba. I played junior hockey for the Brandon Wheat Kings for two years when they were a New York Rangers sponsored team. I guess I went there because of my father. Since he played for New York it was my favorite club as a kid growing up.

The first year I barely made the team, but I hung on. We lost out in the finals to Edmonton. The next year we had a few new faces. Once again, we won the Manitoba Junior Hockey League and went all the way through until we lost out to Edmonton once again. I believe that they beat Niagara Falls for the Memorial Cup that year.

That was the first year that things really fell into place individually. I ended up being one point short of winning the scoring championship. That year in the playoffs we played 19 games and I had 19 goals. As a result, I had four different scholarships offered to me in the States (Denver-Colorado, Michigan Tech., University of Minnesota and North Dakota). I went to North Dakota partially because it was close to home and also because several of the guys I played junior with went there, so I knew they had a good team. At that time they were one of the hockey powers, in fact they won the NCAA championship.

I played there for three years, during which we went to the NCAA tournament one year and lost out. One year we won our

---

[13] Dennis' father Bryan Sr. played in 449 games with the Rangers scoring 187 goals and 175 assists.

league and the next year, I think, we were in second place. We had a good team.

GOING PRO

The road to the NHL from college still isn't as easy as the major-junior route, but back in the late 1960's it was virtually impossible. When Hextall turned pro after his junior year, he was the third player to make it to the National Hockey League via the university route.

After playing in the New York Rangers minor league system for a couple of seasons, Hextall proceeded to be moved around between teams, going from New York to LA to Montreal and then to Oakland. Hextall is probably best remembered for his years in Minnesota and Detroit best, which is where had his best production.

I turned pro coming off of my junior year, going to the Rangers. I think I was the third guy to make it into the NHL from college. Red Berenson, I think, was the first to establish himself and I believe Lou Angotti came out of Michigan Tech.

I played with the Rangers' minor league team for two years and I bounced around and then got traded from New York to LA, LA to Montreal and then Montreal to Oakland (California).

That (Oakland) was the first year I was really given an opportunity to play. We had a horrible hockey club. We were just about last place in the NHL. Once again it was a break for me because I got a lot of ice time. It was the first year I scored 20 goals, which was a milestone back then.

From there I was traded to Minnesota, that summer, for Walt McKechnie and Joey Johnston. So I was on the positive end of a two for one trade. The first year in Minnesota I tore my knee up and didn't play much.

The next year, from the day I went to camp to the day I was traded, I led the club in scoring. We finished in second place behind Chicago. We just couldn't seem to get over the hump. That was when Chicago had Bobby Hull, Stan Makita and Tony Esposito. They had a good team.

Then, just when Minnesota started their downturn, I was traded to Detroit. I was there for four years and then went to Washington and was a player/assistant coach for a year and a half.

When that was finished we moved back to Detroit to live. We knew there were business opportunities there and we had gotten to like the community, so we ended up staying here and we have been here for over 20 years.

YESTERDAY VERSUS TODAY

Dennis looks at today's players and feels that the game was played with more discipline in his days, but doesn't feel that that game has really changed all that much.

I don't think I'd do anything different. I really enjoyed the game. Obviously our game wasn't what it is today, but I think we had more fun.

There were fewer teams in the league. The game was played with a lot tighter checking. If you didn't you weren't around. The discipline was there. You go down and watch the games today and you hear about the left wing lock and all this, and really it's just playing your position and back checking and

Dennis Hextall's NHL career spanned 13 seasons, during which he played in 681 games totaling 153 goals, 350 assists and 1398 penalty minutes.

Photo © 1997 Lawrence P. Nader

playing the game. It's different terminology but I don't think the game has changed much.

I feel that the kids today may skate a little faster and they shoot the puck better overall. We use to have one or two guys who could shoot the puck on every team. I think today there are more guys who can really blister a puck. A lot has to do with the equipment. The equipment is lighter, your sticks are better. Some players use those aluminum shafts, which are a little more consistent.

But, I think as far as the basics they are still a little behind. I don't think the league overall handles the puck as well as years ago. You have some very talented players today, I'm not knocking that, but I think the players have a different attitude, and it's all brought about from the money. It's a big business today. A salary like Steve Yzerman's, for example, would have paid our entire budget 20 years ago.

I don't begrudge the players the money, but I don't like the attitudes of some of the kids today. They won't sign autographs and sort of dump on the public. I think the public is getting dumped on with the high salaries. A lot of people can't afford to go to the games.

It'll go so far and pretty soon the stands will be empty. Baseball really hurt themselves a few years ago and they haven't really recovered, and I'd hate to see hockey do that. I'm not so sure that it's not heading in that direction.

I go back to the old Olympia Stadium. After every game we came out into the corridor and signed autographs. But, today I don't think you can get near the players.

I think when you make that kind of money, and your wealthy, you are a target to the public, so I can see where some of the care has to be taken to keep the players away. But, I also see where some of these kids will not sign autographs unless they are paid substantial dollars.

ON BOBBY ORR

During his career, Hextall played against some of the biggest names in the game. Out of that vast pool of players he selected Bobby Orr as the greatest he ever played against.

I think the best player I played against would have been Bobby Orr. That's not taking anything away from the other great players. When I first broke in, we'd come into Detroit and you'd have Delvecchio centering Howe and Mahovlich, they just wouldn't give you the puck. You had to take your own puck out if you wanted to play hockey, because they had their own game going.

I think Orr controlled the game. He could speed it up or slow it down. He was amazing. He'd be killing the penalty behind your net with the puck and he'd still beat you back down to the other end of the ice. If he had not had those knee injuries, he might have turned out to be the greatest to ever play.

They (Boston) had a great team, but you could have taken anyone off their team, even Phil Esposito, and it wouldn't have the effect as losing Bobby Orr would. In my mind he is the best I ever played against.

HIS RED WINGS DAYS

The irony of Minnesota trading Hextall to Detroit was that prior to the season in which he was traded, he had a clause in his contract that stated he could not be traded to Pittsburgh or Detroit. For whatever reason, he was sent to Detroit.

I enjoyed the game. I didn't care whether we played at home or on the road. I got a lot of laughs and a lot of stories.

When I was in Minnesota I had terms in my contract that said the two cities I couldn't be traded to were Detroit and Pittsburgh. The year after the clause slipped out of my contract Delvecchio trades for me and I end up in Detroit. After I got to the city and met a few people and saw what the city had to offer, I fell in love with it. I've been here for 20-some years now and have no plans on moving.

In Detroit we had a physical team the last couple of years. A lot of people didn't think we could beat anybody, but all of a sudden we ended up in second place behind Montreal (1977-78).

"We had a few donnybrooks that year. We had a half-hour brawl with Toronto one night that I guess I got going. I hit Borje Salming behind the net. The next thing you know couple of guys started coming, Bugsy Watson suckered somebody and we got everybody on the ice having a brawl.

In another Sunday afternoon game, in Philadelphia, Nick Libett, Bryan Watson and myself had their three big tough guys on their back. Mel Bridgeman came off the Philadelphia bench, he was heading to get into the fight, and all of a sudden he realized Danny Maloney was still on our bench. I think he pretty near broke the blades off of his skates making a U-turn at center ice so he wouldn't get Maloney.

I wish I could have played in Detroit a couple of more years. I went down to the parade last year[14] and when you see the way people here support their teams, it's phenomenal. Every one of these kids on the team today has to realize that if they keep their nose clean and work hard everyone in this city will love them.

Dennis Hextall takes a few minutes to plan strategy with ex-teammate Gary Bergman during a Detroit Red Wing Alumni charity game.
Photo © 1997 Lawrence P. Nader

---

[14] 1997 Stanley Cup parade celebrating the Red Wings first championship in 42 years.

DENNIS HEXTALL TODAY

Hextall had a couple of coaching and management offers following his career, but they never seemed quite right to him. As a result he returned to Detroit and has been a partner in a local firm since 1980.

My second year out of hockey I was offered the Red Wing coaching job. They were in the process of firing Wayne Maxner and they called me about the job. I had the job if I took it on their terms. I didn't want to, so I passed on it.

The following year Fred Shero, from the New York Rangers, contacted me. He offered me a three-year contract to be GM and coach of New Haven for two years and go up to the Rangers as an assistant for the third year. My wife and I were actually in New Haven looking for a house about three weeks before the season. After we came back we decided we didn't want to move, so we turned it down.

I joined a firm in Detroit called Maybee Associates. I've been a partner with them since 1980. We are a manufacture rep firm. We've had some ups and downs business-wise but overall we've been fairly successful.

Recently I bought into a company called North Star Manufacturing. It's a small machining shop. A few years ago we were in the red a little bit, but we've turned it around and are making money.

Business is just like in hockey. When someone does something to you, you take a number and go after them. The more business we can take the stronger it makes our company. It's all a part of business. Just like in sports, the companies that work together succeed. Like in hockey, you can have all the stars you want but if you don't play together you aren't going to win.

Hextall remains a member of the Detroit Red Wing Alumni and skates in numerous charity games each season.

DENNIS HEXTALL'S CAREER STATS

Season	Team	League	GP	G	A	Pts	PIM
1964-65	U. of North Dakota	NCAA	33	17	36	53	0
1965-66	U. of North Dakota	NCAA		14	20	34	0
1966-67	Knoxville Knights	EHL	61	20	56	76	202
1967-68	Omaha Knights	CPHL	10	0	2	2	9
1967-68	Buffalo Bisons	AHL	51	15	33	48	114
1968-69	Buffalo Bisons	AHL	60	21	44	65	179
1968-69	NY Rangers	NHL	13	1	4	5	25
1969-70	Springfield-Montreal	AHL	39	15	27	42	178
1969-70	LA Kings	NHL	28	5	7	12	40
1970-71	California Golden Seals	NHL	78	21	31	52	217
1971-72	Cleveland Barons	AHL	5	1	1	2	18
1971-72	Minnesota North Stars	NHL	33	6	10	16	49
1972-73	Minnesota North Stars	NHL	78	30	52	82	140
1973-74	Minnesota North Stars	NHL	78	20	62	82	138
1974-75	Minnesota North Stars	NHL	80	17	57	74	147

DENNIS HEXTALL'S CAREER STATS
(CONT.)

Season	Team	League	GP	G	A	Pts	PIM
1975-76	Minnesota North Stars	NHL	59	11	35	46	93
1975-76	Detroit Red Wings	NHL	17	5	9	14	71
1976-77	Detroit Red Wings	NHL	78	14	32	46	158
1977-78	Detroit Red Wings	NHL	78	16	33	49	195
1978-79	Detroit Red Wings	NHL	20	4	8	12	33
1978-79	Washington Capitals	NHL	26	2	9	11	43
1979-80	Washington Capitals	NHL	15	1	1	2	49
	NHL Totals		**681**	**153**	**350**	**503**	**1398**

Larry Johnston

WHA Career: 1974-75 (1 season)
NHL Career: 1967-1977 (7 seasons)
NHL Teams: Los Angeles Kings, Detroit Red Wings, Kansas City Scouts, Colorado Rockies

Larry Johnston was a hard-nose style player. Those who remember him play, remember him as more of the enforcer on the ice than a scorer. He was a strong, rugged defenseman who made it to the NHL after considerable minor league experience. The 5'11", 195-pound defenseman was one of the guys behind the scenes that created the skating room for the big guns to do their work.

The Kitchener, Ontario naïve escaped serious injury in the 1972-73 season when he was struck in the eye by an opponent's stick. That same season he led the Wings in penalty minutes with 169. Johnston, who turned down an offer to play professional football before choosing hockey, still resides in the Detroit, Michigan area where he is owner/operator of Johnston's Sports Den, as well as a scout for the Calgary Flames.

THE EARLY YEARS

I grew up in Kitchener, Ontario. Kitchener has a good history of producing hockey players. A lot of good hockey players have come out of there. As I was growing up, instead of going away to play major junior I stayed at home and played junior "B". I played about 5 years of junior "B" hockey there, starting when I was fifteen. After being drafted by the Barrie Flyers, a junior "A" team, I decided that I didn't want to play there. I decided that I wanted to stay at home.

I was the property of the Boston Bruins, at that time. In those days there wasn't a draft as there is today. When we were 15 years old, somebody owned us. We signed these "A" cards and "B" cards and different "C" forms and so on. As fourteen or fifteen-year-olds, we just became their property. And I just happened to be the property of the Boston Bruins.

MINOR-PRO YEARS

Like most players, Johnston didn't make the move to the National Hockey League without paying his dues in the minor leagues. In addition to playing for the Johnstown Jets (EHL) and Tulsa Oilers (CPHL), Johnston paid some hard-time playing for Eddie Shore's infamous Springfield Indians.

Boston traded me to the Toronto Maple Leafs as a 19-year-old, and I played in the Eastern Hockey League. That was a learning experience. In those days it was a pretty rugged league, similar to the movie Slap Shot. Believe it or not, that movie was pretty close to the truth. The way they played, every night there were bench-clearing brawls. Travel was tough. You would travel all night, get off the bus and play another game.

As I look back on it today it was a great experience; I had a lot of good times. I probably really and truly learned how to fight while playing in that league. I had a black eye from the start of the season to the end. It was either the right eye or left eye and sometimes both eyes. It was a tough league, with stick swinging and brawls. Usually players didn't get suspended for that kind of stuff.

We'd clear the bench, a couple of guys would get the penalties and we'd go back and do it all over again later. It was a nasty league but I learned a lot. I learned how to take care of myself pretty well.

Then the Maple Leafs sent me to Tulsa, Oklahoma in the Central League, which was a developmental league for the National Hockey League. There were only six teams in the NHL in those days, so each team in the National League had a team in that league. Most of the players there were younger players, first or second year pros, plus three or four older guys to kind of stabilize the young players. That was a fun time in my life.

We use to fly to games. That was a blessing after playing in the East Coast League where you literally got off the bus, went into the rink and played, and got back on the bus. You'd get a bunch of White Castles and a six pack of beer and would eat and drink until you fell asleep. That was good nourishment, right?

I played there for a year and a half and was traded to Springfield, which was an independent team owned by Eddie Shore. I was traded for Bruce Campbell, a goaltender who went to Toronto and played on a couple of Stanley Cup winners. That's when the fun began -- playing for Eddie Shore.

PLAYING FOR EDDIE SHORE

Those who have been around the game for years remember the fear that playing for Shore's Springfield team struck into players. Many NHL teams threatened players with being sent to Springfield if they got out of line. It was a threat that worked more times than not. A fate even worse than playing for Shore's Indians was not playing at all.

If you found yourself on Shore's bad side, you usually wound up in a group called the "Black Aces."[15] In keeping with Shore's maniacal personality, you never knew what you would be doing as a member of the Black Aces. You might be parking cars, selling programs or cleaning up after the game, but one thing was certain though, you knew that you wouldn't be seeing any ice time.

All the stories you hear, just unbelievable stories, most of them are true. I played for Eddie for two and a half years, and

---

[15] The Black Aces were players that for whatever reason had gotten in Shore's doghouse. When he was unhappy with a player they were benched until he deemed otherwise. Reasons for Shore putting you on the Black Aces could range from your on-ice performance all the way to you smiling when he wanted you to frown. Shore was well known around the hockey circuit as a very strange bird.

every day was a new experience. Some days we'd practice 6-8 hours a day and they would never turned the lights on. They had an old rink in Springfield with a lot of skylights. We'd start practicing as soon as it got light enough to light up the building, and you'd better be there.

Guys would come at 8 o'clock in the morning because he might decide that that was when he was going to start a practice. If you weren't there he'd just suspend you. He didn't care who you were, he'd just suspend you.

We probably had 29 or 30 guys on the roster, and we usually had eight or nine guys suspended at all times. That extra group that didn't play were known as the "Black Aces." A lot of the older guys would know what that term meant. The benches were three tiered. The first two tiers were where the guys that were playing sat and the third tier was where the guys sat with their suits on. They were the "Black Aces."

I remember one New Year's Eve, we started practicing about 8 o'clock in the morning and were still practicing at 8 o'clock at night. As the day went on, he (Shore) would send five guys home at a time. The group would continue to get smaller. I was in the last group with Jacque Carron, goaltender Roger Cody and Barclay Plager. We were the last guys on the ice that day. It was unbelievable.

His practices weren't hard. They were boring. You never skated hard. You never did anything hard. There use to be tap dancing, or you'd have to hold you stick a certain way. He would literally tie guys' hands to their sticks. He would tie the goaltenders to the net by tying a skate lace around their neck to the crossbar, so they couldn't go down. He didn't want his goalies going down. If they tried to go down, they'd hang themselves.

We would play a game on a Saturday night and have to go to Quebec for a Sunday night game, so we'd leave right after the game. The game was over at 10:30 and he'd say the bus was going to leave at 12 o'clock in order to give the guys a chance to grab a sandwich. We'll at 11:30 he'd say let's go and only half of the guys were on the bus. The guys that missed the bus were afraid. So they'd get in their cars and they would drive up to Quebec. It was awful.

The players in those days had no power. It was all management. While I was there, out of our 20 regulars, I counted 16 guys that played in the NHL the next year. We had a pretty good team. But what was going on is that he would suspend guys that were rinky-dink, so no one would ever say anything. They were just glad it wasn't them.

But one day he suspended Brian Kilrea, Dale Roelf, and Bill White. These were married guys that had families. When I was there I was single. Now all of a sudden they paid attention to what was going on. With the guys before, they didn't really care.

It was actually a good thing that it happened. What we did was to muster a lot of support. We said that until those guys were reinstated, we weren't playing. Shore's response to that was that we were all suspended.

So we called other teams. The players from these teams said that they wouldn't come to Springfield. If they put a team on the ice, they wouldn't play them. So there was some support building. But after a week we were all getting nervous. We were still young guys and we were worried about our careers. We were sitting a motel room someplace trying to decide what we were going to do. Were we going to stand tall or are we going to go back and play?

Kenny Mosdell Jr., whose dad had played with the Montreal Canadiens, was on the team then. He mentioned a young attorney in Toronto he knew that had just jumped on the seen and was representing Bobby Orr. The guy's name happened to be Alan Eagleson. We called Eagleson and he said 'don't do anything I'll be there tomorrow.' That was probably one of the main things that jumped Eagleson into the limelight.

He came in, went nose to nose with Shore, and solved the problem. That was a big thing then, a pro-team on strike. But Alan Eagleson solved the problem. As I look at him today, with what he turned out doing to the players, I am sorry we called him.[16]

At the end of the year, expansion came along and Shore sold his team and that was the end of the Eddie Shore era. That stuff went on for years and years like that. He would just suspend hockey players and they would just never play hockey again. Today, you'd never get away with that. Back then a lot of teams would threaten players that if they didn't behave, or do something, they would send them to Eddie Shore. Guys didn't want to go there.

Then expansion came along and I was the property of the LA Kings. The LA Kings bought the whole team (Springfield) and most of those players went to LA. I played in LA for a year and was traded to the Detroit Red Wings.

MOVING TO DETROIT

After spending three seasons in the Kings farm system, Johnston found himself part of a 6-man trade between L.A. and the Detroit Red Wings in 1970, and played his first season in the Red Wing organization with the Baltimore Clippers of the AHL. In the 1971-72 season, he started with the Tidewater Wings of the AHL before making it to Detroit, which turned out to be where he played the majority of his NHL career games. Johnston credits Detroit as the city where his NHL career really started.

I was sent to Detroit along with Dale Roelf and Gary Croteau in return for Garry Monahan, Matt Ravlich and Brian Gibbons. That's really when I played my best hockey; when I got a good chance to play in the National Hockey League. It was good experience.

---

[16] Alan Eagleson was charged with racketeering and defrauding NHLPA in a U.S. grand jury indictment that was handed down by in 1994. He was sentenced to 18 months in jail in Jan. 1998 after pleading guilty.

We didn't have much toughness on that team, but we had some good hockey players. I was just happy to be in the NHL. It was the so-called 'Darkness with Harkness' era (Ned Harkness was the Red Wings' General Managers at the time), but in all honesty I didn't look at it that way.

We had a real good hockey team. The first year I was there we had about 76 points and didn't make the playoffs, unfortunately. That was when, with expansion, they had two divisions. Detroit was in the tougher division.

As much as people complained about those teams, the building was always full. We won most of our home games. I think we missed the playoffs by one point. Johnny Wilson was our coach that year. The following year we had 86 points and missed the playoffs again. That's when Johnny was fired.

Then the franchise kind of went into shambles. In 1973-74 season, they hired a coach (Ted Garvin) that lasted 11 games. Alex Delvecchio then took over as coach and Harkness was fired. After Harkness' firing, Alex took over both roles. There was a lot of turmoil in the upper echelon. Anytime that happens it filters down. The guys were choosing up sides. This guy was a Harkness guy, this guy was a Skinner guy. It was bad.

Even though we didn't win anything, those were good years. I was just happy to be there. I was a role player, the so-called tough guy on the team. I had to do all the fighting, which isn't always easy. Every night you know you're going out there to fight the other teams' tough guy. Even when you win the fights you still had lumps on your head the next day, you still hurt a little bit.

I think Johnny Wilson was a good coach. I don't think he was real technical, but he got a lot out of you by being a player's coach. That was the beginning of videotaping and college coaches coming into the league.

Teams in those days had a lot of good players on them. It's not like today where teams have about three good players and rest of the guys are just hard working guys. We had (Marcel) Dionne, (Mickey) Redmond, (Red) Berenson and Delvecchio. I thought we had a good hockey team.

We pretty much played with four defensemen and three lines. The checking line wasn't really a big thing in those days. You really had to play your best against the best. That was about the period that Bobby Orr was in the game, and he changed the defenseman's role. Bobby Orr was the best player I ever played against. He was outstanding. He really controlled the game.

It use to be where the defenseman never got in the play, now they were starting to do that more and more. Then it just kept coming. You would play teams like Boston and they'd come at you four guys at a time. The Rangers had Brad Park who did the same thing. The Montreal Canadiens had Larry Robinson, Guy Lapointe and Serge Savard. They would come at you five at a time. So I was playing when the game was starting to change.

THE WORLD HOCKEY ASSOCIATION

Like many players in the mid-70's, Johnston was talked into making the jump to the WHA with promises of better pay than the players were receiving in the NHL. Johnston didn't have to leave the Detroit area to make the jump, as he signed with Johnny Wilson's Michigan Stags, who played at Detroit's downtown Cobo Arena. The team was short lived, though.

After failing in Los Angeles as the Sharks, the franchise was moved to Detroit where they became known as the Stags. About the midway point of the season, the team packed up and moved to Baltimore. Luckily for Johnston, he had a "out clause." His contract read that if the team was to move from the Detroit area Johnston would be released from his contract.. Unfortunately, however, like many WHA players, Johnston never got paid for his time served.

I left the Wings for the World Hockey Association and signed a big contract with the Michigan Stags. That was a big mistake. I never got paid, as they had no money. The Stags were in Detroit for about 2 month's then they moved to Baltimore. The one thing I had in my contract was that if they ever left Detroit, I became a free agent.

So when they went to Baltimore, I jumped back to the National Hockey League. Johnny Wilson was my coach with the Stags as well. He talked me into going there and it was a bad thing.

We use to head on road trips and, as we were getting on the bus to take us to the airport, the driver wouldn't let us board until he got paid in cash. We would get to the hotel and have to sit in the lobby until they paid for the rooms in cash. That's how they operated.

The first sign I had that there were problems was when I got to training camp and all the sticks were neutrals (straight sticks with no left or right curve). I knew right then that things were bad.

After the Stags moved to Baltimore I signed with the NHL expansion Kansas City Scouts. My connection there was with Sid Abel who was their General Manager. Kansas City was a pretty good town, it was a fun place to play.

Obviously we didn't have a very good hockey team. It was an expansion team with a lot of young kids on it. The coaching was real bad though. It was kind of a disaster in that aspect.

In their second year, they had the same problem that the Wings had; they started going through coaches. They brought in Eddie Bush. The game had passed him by about 10 years before that. The team was only in existence there for two years when the franchise then moved to Colorado. So the following season I finished my career in Colorado.

TOUGH GUYS

Johnston accepted his role as a tough guy when he played. When he suited for a game, he never had any misconceptions that he was going to be the go-to guy on the power play. He knew that his role was to go out, play hard and protect his team's top guns.

There was a lot of tough guys back when I played, and they weren't really know as fighters. They were just tough guys, but when they did fight, they didn't lose.

Larry Robinson was a very tough guy, but didn't fight that much. Clark Gillies was a tough guy. They just played hockey. They didn't want to fight. Personally we'd say 'let the dog sleep.' Don't bother him and he's harmless when he isn't ugly.

In my day I played against the Broad Street Bullies, and they were known for being tough. They had lots of tough guys there. You knew when you played them, it was going to be a tough game. When we would go into Philadelphia, we had guys that would always come up an injury or sickness. It was amazing that it only happened when you played Philadelphia.

AFTER THE GAME

As with all hockey players, the time came where Johnston had to make a decision of whether to continue playing or retire. The decision is never an easy one, and each player has different reason for continuing or leaving the game. Sometimes the player can look back and realize it was the right decision to make, other times he looks back with regrets.

I think the biggest factor in my quitting hockey, was that my kids were going to school. We started moving around, Detroit to Kansas City to Colorado. On top of this, my contract was up. I sat down and decided the best thing for me and my family at the time was that I retire.

Looking back, I wish I didn't. I think that was another bad choice. If you hung on for a couple of more years, with expansion, you could almost play forever. You look at some of the older players playing today, it's because of expansion. You need hockey players and who's better than a guy that played in the league. But, anyway, that was our choice. I didn't know if I wanted to stay in Kansas City, go back to Canada or move back to Detroit.

My wife is from the East Coast and we considered going back there, but we decided to move back to Detroit being it is such a sports town. I thought that was the best place. I had to make a living, so we packed up, moved back to Detroit, and I went to work for Coca-Cola.

I worked for Coca-Cola for ten years. I had a good job there. I worked up through the ranks and ended up being a sales manager. I got restless and tired of working for somebody else, so I decided to buy a bar (Johnston bought a bar on the Detroit border from Eddie Giacomin). Now I am real restless. I've been in the bar business for 12 years. I went from working 40 hours a week to 140.

ROAD TO SCOUT

Using his skills developed by playing the game over the years, Johnston decided to coach for a while. This was an avenue where he felt that he could pass on his knowledge and help youngsters develop their skills. From there he accepted an offer by the Calgary Flames to scout for the NHL franchise.

My kids were playing hockey in Southfield, Michigan (a suburb of Detroit). I went to the rink one day with my oldest boy and the coach asked me if I would help them out a little bit. I said okay, and the next practice I went and helped them out. The following practice I showed up and there was no coach. All of a sudden all of the parents were calling me coach. The other guy had quit, so I kind of got suckered into being the coach and I ended up coaching for 12 years.

Most of those 12 years I coached in the Little Caesers' program, AAA hockey which is very good hockey. That was fun. I pretty much worked with my own son. I coached him and, when he went up to Canada to play for a year, I decided wanted to watch him play and left coaching.

I got out of coaching. I paid my debt back to hockey by coaching for those 12 years. I coached a lot of good kids. It was a lot of fun.

After I was done with coaching for a few years, one of my friends asked me if I was interested in doing some scouting. So I started scouting for the Calgary Flames part time and have been doing that for six years (as of 1999). I enjoy seeing the kids play today. There are a lot of good hockey players in this area (Detroit).

I scout this area mostly. I do the CCHA (Central Collegiate Hockey Association) and the local scene here. I do some junior games with the Plymouth Whalers (OHL), Compuware Tier II (NAHL) and Little Caesers teams. This is a pretty good hockey area. A lot of good kids come out of this area. So I have to be on my toes, I don't want to miss anybody.

HOCKEY TODAY AND BEYOND

Over the years, the game of hockey has changed in many ways. During his years, Johnston has seen many of those changes. He remembers the way the game used to be played and sees the way it is played today. The slugger defenseman likes the way it used to be better.

Hockey came from basically a Canadian game when I played, to an international game today. We have all kinds of Europeans and North Americans playing. The game is faster today then when I played, but I don't particularly like the way it's played today. They shoot the puck in and chase it.

You don't see the great plays that you use to see in the older days. Guys like (Stan) Makita, Billy Harris and (Phil) Esposito would carry the puck in and make plays. I'd like to see the game change, but I have no idea what rule changes would make it better. I would try to eliminate some of the shooting in and chasing so people could see a little bit more play making.

The dump and chase has taken a lot away from the game. You shoot it in, the goaltender goes back and stops it and then shoots it back out. Everybody comes back and regroups then they shoot it back in. The goaltender is more a part of the game now then he ever was. When I played, the goaltender stayed in the goal crease. I think they should make the goalie stay in the crease. At least when you shoot it in you'd have a chance to get the puck.

Today you get the good goaltender, and they're lots of them, the Roy's and Hextall's, and they come out to play the puck and they fire it down the ice. They can score a goal if you have an empty net.

I'd also like to see more play making. The guys like (Wayne) Gretzky could still do that. Gretzky didn't shoot the puck in. He never did. He played old-time hockey his whole career. He carried the puck, made plays and the guys that played with him score goals.

Teams have such a shortage of real good players. If you look at the real good players, they'll still carry the puck in. (Steve) Yzerman will carry the puck in and try to make plays. (Mario) Lemieux did when he still played in Pittsburgh. (Jaromir) Jagr does it. Gretzky does it. (Pavel) Bure will do it. (Thereon) Fluery in Calgary does too. They don't shoot and chase, they try to carry the puck in. The use their speed and stick-handling ability to do that.

This all started after expansion when a bad team was playing a good team, there was such a difference in play. You take the Kansas City Scouts playing the Montreal Canadiens. They had four good lines and we didn't. So how would you play against teams like that and not get blown out? You dump it out and shoot it in. That's what all the bad teams did. From there it became the game. From there it just snowballed.

LARRY JOHNSTON'S CAREER STATS

Season	Team	League	GP	G	A	Pts	PIM
1963-64	Johnston Jets	EHL	71	7	39	46	356
1964-65	Tulsa Oilers	CPHL	57	4	16	20	262
1965-66	Tulsa Oilers	CPHL	36	2	6	8	129
1965-66	Springfield Indians	AHL	29	2	5	7	58
1966-67	Springfield Indians	AHL	59	4	14	18	93
1967-68	Springfield Kings	AHL	60	2	22	24	197
1968-69	Los Angeles Kings	NHL	4	0	0	0	4
1969-70	Fort Worth Wings	CHL	13	1	0	1	60
1969-70	Springfield Kings	AHL	52	3	24	27	150
1970-71	Baltimore Clippers	AHL	58	2	14	16	198
1971-72	Tidewater Wings	AHL	12	1	1	2	45
1971-72	Detroit Red Wings	NHL	65	4	20	24	111
1972-73	Detroit Red Wings	NHL	73	1	12	13	169
1973-74	Detroit Red Wings	NHL	65	2	12	13	139
1974-75	Michigan Stags	WHA	49	0	9	9	93

LARRY JOHNSTON'S CAREER STATS
(CONT.)

Season	Team	League	GP	G	A	Pts	PIM
1975-75	Kansas City Scouts	NHL	14	0	7	7	10
1975-76	Kansas City Scouts	NHL	72	2	10	12	112
1976-77	Maine Nordiques	NAHL	51	4	22	26	62
1976-77	Colorado Rockies	NHL	25	0	3	3	35
	WHA Totals		**49**	**0**	**9**	**9**	**93**
	NHL Totals		**318**	**9**	**64**	**73**	**580**

Nick Libett

NHL Career: 1967-81 (14 Seasons)
NHL Teams: Detroit Red Wings, Pittsburgh Penguins

Stepping onto the ice for his first NHL game in 1967, Nick Libett had no idea how long his career would last or that he would remain with the Red Wings for 12 of his 14 NHL seasons and end up calling Detroit his home.

Libett played for Detroit until 1979 when he was dealt to the Pittsburgh Penguins for NHL veteran Pete Mahavolich who returned to the Wings for his second go round.

Libett went on to play for the Penguins through the 1980-81 season before calling it quits. Libett continues to make Detroit his home.

YOUNGER DAYS

Nick Libett grew up in Stratford, Ontario and was a product of the Stratford Public Schools hockey system at an early age. He then went on to play Pee-Wee, Bantam and Midget in the Stratford system before moving on to play four years of junior 'A' in Kitchener.

I was born and raised in Stratford, Ontario. I grew up through the Stratford minor hockey system. In those days they had Pee Wee, Bantam, Midget and Juvenile hockey. I never played Juvenile hockey, but a lot of guys did. Juvenile was post-midget hockey. The guys that played juvenile were about 17 to 18-year-olds and were not really going to go on to anyplace.

They also had public school hockey, which is where I started, like most everybody. It was kindergarten through eighth grade. One of my first recollections was when I was in the first grade playing width-wise on the rink at the Stratford Arena. They had three games going at one time. That was how you first started back then. You played your public school hockey on Saturday mornings.

I was always on All-Star teams and those teams always played up a level. There was a Pee Wee All-Star team and a Pee Wee League and, a Bantam All-Star team and a Bantam league. You always played up a level. The Pee Wee All-Stars always played in the Bantam league and the Bantam All-Stars always played in the midget house league. So if you were one of the better caliber players you were always playing up your age level.

In our public school hockey we would sometimes practice 7 to 8 am prior to school. You'd be so excited about going to practice you couldn't sleep. We'd play our games on Saturday morning and then we'd get on the streets and play road hockey for hours. We never had the thermal equipment they have now. You'd have a jacket and you'd put gloves on and socks with rubber boots and go out and play. It's amazing none of us lost our toes or fingers to frostbite. It use to bother us when the sand trucks came down the street cause you had too much friction, you couldn't slide with your boots on.

I remember Jimmy Skinner and Johnny Graham, they were scouts for Detroit, coming to my house when I was 12-years-old. In those days what they would do was to sponsor a minor hockey system. In another words, give them $1,000 if they saw a couple of boys that they thought might make the National League. I was one of them, as well as, two other guys, Henry Montieth and Moe Morris. The Red Wings basically sponsored our system, which gave them first dibs on us. The only commitment was that they (Detroit) might get the option of us going to Hamilton, which Detroit ran, to play junior hockey at 16 or 17-years-old.

You didn't have to do that but if they gave you hockey gloves and golf clubs, and your parents got three or four hundred dollars a year, that was big time back then. It was a big enticement. It was a different structure than what you have today. My parents never had a car so I would throw the bag over my shoulder and walk to the arena.

Today, triple "A" hockey seems to be high-powered, high-pressured hockey. It didn't seem to be like that when we were growing up.

I went to Hamilton when I was 15 to play junior "B", but I got homesick and came home that year. I just didn't like it; I just wasn't ready. So I came home and played midget.

The next year, when I was 16, I went to Hamilton and played junior "A" with the Hamilton Red Wings. I played four years in Hamilton and went to school there. When I played with Hamilton, Pit Martin, Paul Henderson, Bobby Wall and Gary Doak were also on the team.

MOVING TO THE PROS

Libett's road to the National Hockey League wasn't without paying his dues in the minor leagues. Following his junior 'A' days in Hamilton, Libett headed to Cincinnati, Ohio to play for the Cincinnati Wings of the Central Professional Hockey League.

The following two seasons he played in Memphis when the Cincinnati franchise moved their roots to Tennessee. From there he played for the San Diego Gulls in the Western Hockey League and the Fort Worth Wings back in the CPHL before getting his break with Detroit.

While I was playing in Hamilton, I went south with Jimmy Peters Jr. and played three games with Cincinnati in the Central League. He was 18 and I was seventeen and we were playing professional games against guys that were 30-35 years old. We were just kids.

My first year really playing pro was 1966. I was just turning 21. I played that year in Memphis, Tennessee in the Central League. That was the year I got married. I played one year in the Central League. I played a portion of the next year in San Diego and Fort Worth before coming to Detroit, which I think was in January or February, and stayed up here ever since.

In those days, when you turned pro for Detroit you either went to Pittsburgh in the American Hockey League or Memphis in the Central. Pittsburgh being in the American Hockey League had a little older crew. So, the guys from Hamilton and Edmonton, the Detroit sponsored junior teams, ended up in Memphis.

What I remember most about my early days in Memphis, in addition to getting married, was the difference in ages. We had guys that were 21 and then we had guys that were 35 on the team. Alex Faulkner for example played on that team. Andre Pronovost, who played for Montreal and Detroit, was 35. That's a big age spread when you are young. But overall it was a younger league. It was kind of a glorified junior league. You were getting paid, albeit not much, but you just wanted to play. You knew that was your stepping stone to play in the National League.

THE RED WINGS

It was while he was with Fort Worth that Libett got his call to The Show. After scoring 39 points (11-28) in 40 games with the Texas club, the young left winger was called up to Detroit for the final 22 games of their 1967-68 season. He remained a Wing until being traded to Pittsburgh in 1979.[17]

A product of Stratford, Ontario's minor hockey system, Nick Libett went on to play in 14 NHL seasons – 12 of them in a Detroit Red Wing uniform. His final two years were as a Pittsburgh Penguin.

Photo © 1997 Lawrence P. Nader

---

[17] Libett was sent to the Penguins in exchange for Pete Mahovlich.

I was playing in Fort Worth, in the Central League, When they called me up. I figured I was coming up for a five-game tryout. Detroit was struggling and they were close to the playoffs. It was the first year of expansion. I came up and ended up staying in Detroit for 13 years.

When I came up, guys like Normie Ullman, Paul Henderson and Gordie Howe were on the team. Sid Abel was coaching. The thing that amazed me about coming up was that I had grown up watching these guys.

I remember that Norm Ullman loved the ice, and he loved to play. He worked his butt off. Sid kept yelling at him to get off the ice because he was staying on to long, but he just thrived on it. About two weeks after I arrived, was when they made the trade with Toronto sending Ullman, Henderson and Floyd Smith to the Maple Leafs for Frank Mahovlich, Gary Unger, Carl Brewer and Peter Stemkowski. In hindsight that was a good trade for both teams.

Unfortunately the team was devastated in the early 70's when Ned Harkness took over. He just traded all those guys away and it took a long time to rebuild this franchise. I was the only guy left from the earlier team and I kept waiting to get traded. I was younger, in my early 20's at the time. I guess either no one wanted me or I was too valuable to trade.

I remember one time playing in Chicago, the first game of the year, their trainer was in the room and I was early for the game. He said, 'Nick, you're coming to Chicago. You for Doug Jarret.' I said fine. But you get pumped up for that. You keep thinking 'when's it going to happen?' Well it never happened. Those were frustrating years.

In 1967 when I came to Detroit, we had a good team. The year before this all happened, we had 96 points and ended up in third place. I believe Chicago beat us out in four straight. Every game was 4-2. You think that next year you can build on that. Well, next year they made the coaching change, Ned came in and it was the wrong place at the wrong time. Maybe his style would have worked twenty years later but it didn't work in that day and age.

I can't understand whatever the reason, how one man had that kind of authority. A guy named Jim Bishop came in as a kind of assistant general manager and proceeded to have a lot of authority, as well. They just went through the team, making trades. It was not a good time.

Then Marcel Dionne came to the Red Wings. He eventually became a franchise player for the L.A. Kings, but he could have been Detroit's franchise player. Marcel was a very good hockey player and opinionated. He was very strong willed. He had a conflict, and I'm not exactly sure why he wanted to be traded, but it worked out well for him. We got two very good hockey players for Marcel in Danny Maloney and Terry Harper, but they were not franchise-type players. Marcel never took L.A. to a Stanley Cup but he might have taken Detroit to one. That's how I feel. They could have built around Marcel. It was one of the poorer moves they made, because players like that don't come around very often.

MEMORABLE TIMES AND PLAYERS

While Libett never won the NHL's Holy Grail in his career, he would not have traded his time in the big league for anything in the world. In his day he played with and against some of hockey's greatest names. None stick out in his mind more than Boston's Bobby Orr.

Obviously I never won a Stanley Cup. That's something everyone wished they had. There are lots of good players, Hall of Famers even, that don't have Stanley Cups.

Bobby Orr was a great player. When you played against him you almost wanted to be a spectator. He was that good. You kind of put him in another area because of his ability. You'd say, 'I skate, I shoot, I pass the puck, but boy he sure does it a lot better.'

Watching Bobby Hull come down the ice and shoot the puck the way he did and watching a guy like Frank Mahovlich wind up and shoot the puck were thrilling moments, as well. I grew up watching them on TV and I ended up playing against them and with them.

Just playing in the League and playing in an All-Star game was a highlight. You don't understand how good the superstars are when you are playing against them individually on a team. But, when you get them all on one team, as in the All-Star game, you see how easy they make the game.

ON RETIRING

For many players, leaving the game is a hard decision. While many know their time to move on has come, it is usually still hard to cut the laces. For Libett, playing in one city for the majority of his career help the transition.

For me there was no decision to retire. I was fortunate to play in one city for a long time and you get to meet a core of people outside of hockey. I was also fortunate to meet some people in the business world that started me in the automobile business, selling to the industry. I started doing this in 1975 with a company called Wyandotte Paint. I started working with them in the summers. I didn't do much in the winter time because of hockey but the next summer I'd come back and do a little bit of work in their lab and began calling on Chrysler to make an in road.

Then when I retired from hockey in 1981, I just went to work. There was no transition for me at all as far as wondering what I was going to do.

PLAYERS TODAY

As a player who has seen the game of the late 1960's change to the game of the 21st century, Libett has his own feelings and opinions on what is right and what is wrong with the sport as it heads into the year 2000 and beyond.

I think the players today are bigger. They are more dedicated to working out and keeping in shape year round. We use to go to training camp for six weeks and that would be our conditioning period. We wouldn't let ourselves go in the summer mind you, but you wouldn't run and lift weights either.

But the biggest difference I see, between then and now, is the style of play. When we played Montreal, for example, my function was to keep Guy Lafleur off the scoresheet. He was a 50-plus goal scorer every year and I was deemed to be a checker who could skate and play my position. But, I'd also get 20-25 goals a year.

Nowadays, if you are a checker and you get 5 or 8 goals, you had a great year. That's what I don't quite understand. If I got 8 goals when I played, I'd be devastated. Even though we had goals scorers who were scoring 40 or 50 goals, I felt my job was to keep the other guys off the ice but still contribute.

Today a lot of the guys don't use their skating ability. I was watching a game recently in Toronto and one of the Leaf players was coming around the net, and was literally a stick's length away from the player ahead of him. Instead of skating, which he could have done because he had momentum on his side, he started coasting and he hooked the guy up around the shoulder and got a penalty. All he had to do was to take two more strides and he could have rode the guy off the puck with his body. That's the biggest difference I see.

I think if the ice surface was made bigger, it would eliminate a lot of the hooking and grabbing. Your skating would become more of a contributor to the game.

There was a game a couple of weeks ago between Detroit and Philadelphia, it was a 1-0 game. It was a terribly boring game. All the play at center ice looked like etch-a-sketch to me. There was no flow up and down the ice. There was no flow in the center zone. It's all that trap, or the hooking, or interference. In the older days, if you cut into the center zone and had your head down, a guy hit you with a good bodycheck. That was part of the program. Now if you do that, you are almost deemed to be a dirty hockey player because you are trying to end someone's career. If somebody is stupid enough to come into the center zone with their head down and you have an opportunity to hit them...so be it.

BATTLING CANCER

Nick Libett never had a bigger fight on or off the ice then he did in 1988. Well after retiring, the feisty Libett found that he had stomach cancer. Never one to back down from a fight, Libett battled the disease and, to date, has kept the lymphoma at bay. He continues to play with the Red Wings Alumni in charity games and from looking at him one would never guess he ever had any such condition.

It was about 1988. I was in Philadelphia on business. Wayne Gretzky had gotten some tickets so I could take my customers to the L.A. – Philadelphia game. Wayne was playing for L.A at the time. I took my customers to the game and remember that I was feeling a little tired that night.

The following weekend I went with my son to a hockey tournament in Buffalo. I had some signs, like my stool was not the right color. It was black.

So, I went to the doctor and that was when they determined that I

Despite battling non-Hodgkin's lymphoma in 1988, Nick Libett remains active on the ice with the Red Wing Alumni. Nearly 12 years later, Libett remains in good health.

Photo © 1997 Lawrence P. Nader

had a tumor in my stomach. It was non-Hodgkin's lymphoma.[18] It was the same as what Jackie Kennedy died of.

It's kind of a paradox – if you get it, it's bad news but the good new is that it's more easily treated. It has a tendency to come back on you in life depending on what stage you get it at. I was in a 1 ½ or 2 stage out of 5 stages, which is good. I had surgery and radiation and here I am eleven-plus years later and still kicking.

I lost about 50 pounds in three months. I use to play at about 195. I went down to 145 and looked like skin and bones. What the radiation did to me was to take my hockey muscle. From playing hockey all those years you develop leg and buttock muscle and all that just kind of went away. Right now, I'm 165 to 170 pounds. I don't grind when I play hockey anymore but I am healthy and everything, as we speak, is fine.

Athletes are supposed to be invincible as far as illnesses. I'm not sure how life threatening it was. My surgery was over 6 hours, it was supposed to last about four. They had a little bit of a problem, whatever it was I don't even know to this day. But, everything worked out.

OLYMPIA STADIUM AND OTHER BARNS

During his career, Libett played in several of the older "barns" as well as many of the newer arenas that were being built in the late 1970's. Nick provides his thoughts on the arenas and how they stack up against the barns of hockey's earlier days.

In retrospect, even though we had some bad years in Detroit, missing the playoffs a number of times, I stayed in Detroit all

---

[18] Non-Hodgkin's Lymphoma is a group of malignancies of lymphoid tissue (lymph nodes, spleen, and other organs). The cancers vary from indolent disease to rapidly progressive cancer. The cause is unknown, but it may be associated with suppression of the immune system, especially after organ transplantation. The tumors are graded according to their level of malignancy; low grade, intermediate grade, or high grade.

these years. I could have demanded to be traded, but I didn't. I just liked the area, the city and the people. It worked out well. It's a good area. It's a good city to play in – win, lose or draw.

Olympia was a special, unique place. My son never saw Olympia. I took him to Chicago Stadium a year or two before it closed, and he was fortunate enough to play in the Boston Gardens in a Hockey East (in college) finals game. But the new arenas just don't have personality.

My question to the architects who build these new arenas is why can't they build them similar to the old arenas but with the newness. The round building with everything being symmetrical just doesn't work for me. I was in Toronto's Maple Leafs Gardens a while back and just walking in there was like getting shivers. It's not built for comfort, but it's just the flavor. The new rinks just don't have any personality. The Montreal Forum was a classic. It was just a great old arena.

When people went to Olympia it was an event. It was like going to your local neighborhood bar. Everybody in the sections knew each other. You could access the refreshment stands with no problem. Everyone was on a first name basis. Now you can tell who's in town by whether the season ticket holder is there or if they are the 'pass me downs'. These new arenas just don't have that flavor.

RED WINGS ALUMNI

Libett continues to stay in good shape and continues play each season with the Red Wing Alumni in various charity games in and around Michigan. The Alumni even schedules a yearly event in Vail, Colorado in which the Alumni members spend the weekend skiing and playing in a charity hockey game. In addition, each winter, a golf week is scheduled to Florida where the members get away from the Michigan winter and relax in the sun for the week, playing golf each day. All in all it keeps them young.

(Playing with the Alumni) doesn't so much keep you physically young, because we don't skate hard enough to really do that. We have practice at Joe Louis Arena about once a week and we have a good workout then. The games don't give us a real good workout because they are all for charity and usually against teams where the guys don't play that well. But the big benefit is mental health. We're together, goofing around, having a sandwich and a beer after and it's the same old stuff you talk about.

Joe Klukay and Jimmy Peters are 76. 'If it wasn't for the Alumni.' Joe has said numerous times, 'I'd be dead. I wouldn't know what to do'. It's a mental health thing, it really is. Our wives sometimes worry, but after 32 years this is the way I am. I'm not going to stop doing it. This is part of what I do. Our common denominator is that most of the guys played in the National Hockey League. We can all relate to the stories even if they're 20 or 30 years old. We've all kind of been there. It's really a close-knit group of guys.

We do a lot of good for the community as far as raising money for charities. A lot of other alumni clubs, play for pay. They get cash in the pocket. We don't do that. We get a beer and a sandwich after the game, and expenses covered. The fee we get for the games, all gets doled out to various charities in the area.

One of our concerns is that as we all get older, the guys (current Red Wings) that live here now will not stay here and the Alumni could go the way of the carrier pigeon. One night in 1997, when Joey Kocur was in between teams, he was living back in Detroit and he played with us. I believe it was in Lemington or Windsor, Ontario, Joey played goal for us. We need guys like that.

There are a number of guys that play for us that were never in the NHL or were on other NHL teams. We are lucky to have those guys because without them we probably wouldn't have an alumni team. Guys like Steve Yzerman and others would be great for the Alumni. People enjoy coming out to see the guys that wore the uniform.

NICK LIBETT'S CAREER STATS

Season	Team	League	GP	G	A	Pts	PIM
1963-64	Cincinnati Wings	CPHL	3	0	2	2	0
1965-66	Memphis Wings	CPHL	4	1	0	1	2
1966-67	Memphis Wings	CPHL	62	12	18	30	30
1967-68	San Diego Gulls	WHL	10	4	2	6	0
1967-68	Fort Worth Wings	CPHL	40	11	28	39	22
1967-68	Detroit Red Wings	NHL	22	2	1	3	12
1968-69	Detroit Red Wings	NHL	75	10	14	24	34
1969-70	Detroit Red Wings	NHL	76	20	20	40	39
1970-71	Detroit Red Wings	NHL	78	16	13	29	25
1971-72	Detroit Red Wings	NHL	77	31	22	53	50
1972-73	Detroit Red Wings	NHL	78	19	34	53	56
1973-74	Detroit Red Wings	NHL	67	24	24	48	37
1974-75	Detroit Red Wings	NHL	80	23	28	51	39
1975-76	Detroit Red Wings	NHL	80	20	26	46	71
1976-77	Detroit Red Wings	NHL	80	14	27	41	25

NICK LIBETT'S CAREER STATS
(CONT.)

Season	Team	League	GP	G	A	Pts	PIM
1977-78	Detroit Red Wings	NHL	80	23	22	45	46
1978-79	Detroit Red Wings	NHL	68	15	19	34	20
1979-80	Pittsburgh Penguins	NHL	78	14	12	26	14
1980-81	Pittsburgh Penguins	NHL	44	6	6	12	4
NHL Totals			**983**	**237**	**268**	**505**	**472**

John Ogrodnick

NHL Career: 1979-1993 (14 seasons)
NHL Teams: Detroit Red Wings, Quebec Nordiques, New York Rangers

John Ogrodnick played 14 seasons in the NHL and enjoyed scoring success averaging a little under one point per game. During his professional career the scoring forward managed three seasons of 30-plus goals, three seasons of 40-plus goals and one 50-goal pinnacle.

Growing up in Alberta, Canada provided a young Johnny O with ample opportunity and ice time to sharpen his skills and bring his game to the level required for continued advancement. Working his way through midgets, Tier II and juniors, Ogrodnick always found a way to make that next step up the hockey ladder eventually being drafted by the Detroit Red Wings in 1979.

Playing for three teams in his career, Ogrodnick was lined with a number of very good players during his career. His job was to jump into the hole and they would find him with the puck. The result was usually a red-light special. In 928 NHL games, Ogrodnick scored 402 goals among 827 points. In his 14-year career, Ogrodnick played in five NHL All-Star games and was voted to the NHL's First All-Star Team in the 1984-85 season.

YOUNG JOHNNY O

While Ogrodnick was born in Ottawa, Ontario in 1959, he was raised in Alberta on an Air Force Base north of Edmonton. With little else to do in the long Alberta winters, Ogrodnick focused on honing his skills in the game of hockey, moving through the youth programs into midget and then on to major-junior hockey.

I was raised on an Air Force Base north of Edmonton in a town called Cold Lake, Alberta. I grew up there from the ages of 5 to 15. Obviously hockey was the predominate sport up there as we had really long winters. It was nice though. We had several outdoor rinks in the area that the military personnel maintained, in addition to one indoor rink.

It was also so cold there that when the snow was compacted enough, we could actually play street hockey with our skates on. It was really cold and hockey was the thing to do. The baby boom was happening so we never had a problem finding enough kids to play hockey.

I was a late grower. I didn't start growing until I was about 14 or 15 years old. I remember that I use to play defense and they had to move me up to forward because I was too small. So I moved from an offensive type defenseman to the forward position.

When I was 15, we ended up moving to Edmonton and that was when my hockey game began to take off. I received a lot more exposure playing midget AA hockey there, even though I only played a half season due to a broken leg. Not being able to play really showed me how much I loved the game and how much I missed playing it. The following season, my final year of midget AA, was when I finally started to really score goals.

MAJOR JUNIOR HOCKEY AND MEMORIAL CUPS

Contrary to how it looks sometimes, very few players actually make it to the major-junior level of the game. Even fewer make it to the NHL. Today with the expansion of the 1990's there is a bigger need than ever before for quality players at the National League level. Back in the late 1970's there were 22 teams and the draft was only six rounds deep, so players really needed to prove themselves during their junior career if the wanted to taken high in the draft.

After midget AA, I ended up going to the New Westminster Bruins' hockey camp when I was 17. It was before they allowed under age players to play in major juniors, so I ended up playing my first year with their Tier II team in Maple Ridge, British Columbia which was about 30-45 miles east of Vancouver. I had a lot of fun down there and it was a good experience. That was the first time I scored 50 goals.

I remember getting called up to play with New Westminster of the Western Hockey League for the playoffs that year after our season in Maple Ridge was over. We (New Westminster) finished up winning the Memorial Cup that year (1977). The series was in Vancouver and it was quite an experience for me, I think that was the first time I ever played on national television. We had a pretty good team. Our defense was very strong, we had Brad Maxwell, Barry Beck, and a few others I can't remember offhand.

The following year I played the full year in major juniors, scoring 50 goals that year as well. We did a lot of traveling through western Canada in juniors and I remember having to tape garbage bags over the bus windows in order to insulate them a little when we went up to Flin Flon, Manitoba because of how cold it is up there. We would play two quick games over the weekend and get out of there as soon as possible. We use to get spanked every time we were up there.

Compared to the Ontario Hockey League and Quebec Major Junior Hockey League we really had a lot of traveling. We had 2 two-week road trips throughout the season. We traveled and bussed all through western Canada. Some of those trips were 12-14 hours long. Our longest trip was from Vancouver to Billings, Montana. I don't recall how many hours it was but it was a very long trip. We ended up winning the Memorial Cup again that year (1978), which was nice.

In my final year of junior, guys like Brian Propp and Ray Allison with the Brandon Wheat Kings were getting a ton of ice time and racking up 150 points. I met with our coach, who at the time was Ernie McLain, about my ice time. There were a number of times that I wasn't being used on the power play. He told me, 'John, we have about nine or ten 19-year-olds that have to get drafted. Don't worry, you'll go in the first round. I am trying to get these other guys stats up so that I can get them drafted.' So I said okay. While Propp and Allison were getting 150 points, my numbers dropped off that last year as a result. I still had a good season, but not as good as it could have been.

I was by the radio on draft day in 1979 and the first round went by followed by the second and third rounds, and I still wasn't picked. I was finally taken in the fourth round by the Detroit Red Wings.[19] At the time I was playing for him, I didn't realize that Ernie was a part time scout for Detroit in addition to his coaching."

You always want to move up to the top of the game, but you don't really ever expect it. I remember playing midget AA and going to see some Tier II hockey games and thinking to myself that I would never be able to play in that league. Then I remember watching the Edmonton Oil Kings playing major-junior and thinking they were so huge. I was standing by the glass thinking it was awesome but you think they are so big that you cannot compete with them. Then, all of a sudden, you end up playing in that league. It is a great feeling. It is amazing the amount of players you play with even in Tier II that never make it up to the next level. You think they are good hockey players but they don't always make it up to that next level.

When I was playing major-junior, I went to watch the Vancouver Canucks play. I was watching the New York Rangers in the pre-game warm-up and saw Nick Fotiu skating. His hockey gloves barely went over his wrists. He was huge. I remember looking at the other players and how big they were and how they moved the puck and thinking there was no way I would be able to play with these guys.

The Coliseum didn't have their ice in time for the teams to practice, so the Rangers ended up practicing at the barn where we played. I remember watching their practice and seeing Phil Esposito and some of the guys. You are just in awe with the way

---

[19] Brian Propp was taken 14th overall by the Philadelphia Flyers while the Hartford Whalers selected Ray Allison with the 18th pick.

these guys can skate and move the puck around. At the time you just don't think you can make it. But eventually you acclimate yourself to that level.

MAKING THE WINGS

Draft day is an exciting time for a young junior player, but it is also one that can bring about nightmares. There is no real guarantee that because you play well and have a successful junior career that you will be drafted high, or even at all. Then, once a player is drafted, there are no guarantees that he will actually play in the NHL or, if he does that he will play there long. Ogrodnick worked hard and was able to form an on-ice chemistry with some good players, helping him to achieve his goals.

I knew a lot of ex-New Westminster players wound up playing for the Wings farm club in Kalamazoo, Michigan. I just made a promise to myself that I wasn't going to be one of those guys that ended up playing in Kalamazoo.

The draft only went six rounds that year. They had just started the underage rule, which said if you were 19 and going to be selected in the draft, they had to be taken in the first

During his 14-year NHL career, John Ogrodnick played for the Detroit Red Wings, Quebec Nordiques and New York Rangers, scoring 402 goals and 425 assists in 928 games.

Photo © 1998 Lawrence P. Nader

round. They didn't take 18 year olds then so it only applied if you were 19. I was 20. That was the draft that (Mark) Messier went as well as (Mike) Gartner, so it was actually a pretty good draft. Some of the guys that were not selected that year actually made out. They were considered free agents and did pretty well with negotiating their contacts.

I had a pretty good camp my first year with Detroit, but they had their line-up pretty much slated. Mike Foligno was their first round draft pick that year, so he was destined to stay there. As a result I started in the minors with their Adirondack farm club in Glen Falls, New York my first year.

Here I am a kid that was raised in Western Canada and I hear I am going to New York. I was all excited. I was thinking it was like New York City. When we pulled into Glen Falls, my first comment was, 'This is it!?' But it turned out to be a beautiful resort area. I only spent three months there before getting called up in January of 1980, but the guys that were down there started to utilize the ski hills and other things the area had to offer. They had a lot of off ice activities.

While Ogrodnick was only in Adirondack a short time, it was long enough to meet his wife BettyAnne before getting the call-up to Detroit.

I remember when I was called up. George Lyle had blown his knee out while playing on the left side with (Dale) McCourt and (Mike) Foligno. Before I left Adirondack, I was at the rink and Ned Harkness told me, 'Good luck and we'll see you back in a few days." I didn't think that was the appropriate thing to say. So I worked hard once I got up there and ended up staying in Detroit.

When I got to the Wings, they put me on the line with McCourt and Foligno. That really worked out great. We really had immediate chemistry and the line worked well. Ted Lindsay was the general manager at that time and he noticed that I was getting a lot of scoring opportunities but because of my being a rookie, I wasn't finishing enough. I played in 41 games that year and only scored 8 goals with 24 assists. The following year, when I played the full season there, I ended up scoring 35 goals and 35 assists.

Ogrodnick started his career with the Wings at a point when the franchise had reached their pinnacle of mediocrity. The team finished last in their division for five years straight (78-79 through 82-83) and, even when they did manage to finish in middle of the pack in 83-84 and 84-85, they were unable to enjoy any real playoff success. Then in 85-86, just when fans thought it could not get any worse, disaster struck and the team could manage no more than 40 points in their 57-loss season. The team went through two coaches that year as Harry Neal manned the bench for the first 35 games (8-23-4) before Brad Park took over for the final 45 games (9-36-2).[20] Jacques Demers took over as head coach for the 1986-87 season.

During his 8 seasons in Detroit, Ogrodnick saw the Red Wings go through eight different coaches – Bobby Kromm, Marcel Pronovost, Ted Lindsay, Wayne Maxner, Nick Polano, Harry Neal, Brad Park and Jacques Demers.

Initially I was excited to be playing in the NHL but obviously, over time, playing in losing situations were tough. We went through a lot of coaches. The team was weak but on the positive side, I was able to get an opportunity to play right away and things started to work out for me on a personal level. On a team level, there is no question about it, we were hurting.

Shortly after I scored 35 goals in my first full season with the Wings, McCourt and Foligno were traded to Buffalo and we were once again really hurting up the middle. The following season I dropped down to 28 goals. Then they made one of the best trades they have ever made, as far as I was concerned anyway, picking up Ivan Bolderiv from Vancouver.

Bolderiv had already been in the league for about 10 or 12 years, but he was a very smooth center ice man. He had a good powerful stride. In talking to our defensemen at the time, they were very intimidated by Bolderiv when they did one-on-ones in

---

[20] The Red Wings 1985-86 season was a franchise record for their worst season ever, as Detroit finished with 40 points (17-57-6).

practice. Ivan was very good at carrying the puck up ice and drawing guys towards him to open up a hole for me. I ended up scoring 42 goals in 83-84 and he was a big part of that.

He really opened up the lanes for me. My job was to find the holes and get into them. When I saw an opportunity where there was a breakdown in the opposition's defensive game, I would capitalize on that, get into the hole and hopefully get the puck. Bolderiv and I click very well that way.

In 1983, they drafted Steve Yzerman.[21] Obviously he has had a fantastic career and isn't finished yet, but at 18 he was young and green. He didn't have the savvy that Bolderiv had at that time. Eventually we ended up having a good line with Ron Dugay on the right side of Yzerman and myself. Overtime we started to show some chemistry there. That was when I had my 40 and 50 goal seasons. Late in the 83-84, I broke my wrist with something like 16 games left in the season. I was sure to hit 50 goals, as I only needed 8 more goals in those remaining games.

My wife was pregnant with our first daughter KelseyAnne at the time and I spent six weeks at home waiting for my wrist to heal. Then a couple of days after I got back into action we went on the road for the playoffs and she went into labor. I was really disappointed because I had been sitting around all those weeks and then I ended up missing our daughter's birth.

In 1986 Detroit management ended up getting rid of Dugay and was starting to mix the lines when Adam Oates came into the picture. Out of all of them, and they are all pretty good hockey players, Oates was the guy that if you got into the hole, you knew you were going to get the puck. He had eyes in the back of his head and he moved the puck very well. We clicked well together. While they continued to juggle the lines, I played with either Yzerman or Oates.

As time moved on you could see Yzerman developing into the player that he became. As far as his leadership, he was a young captain but he was quiet and led the team with his effort on the ice. He came into a bad situation too when he first came

---

[21] Steve Yzerman was taken with Detroit's first pick (4th overall) in the 1983 NHL Entry Draft.

here. It was a losing situation and I know he was deeply frustrated.

It gets tough when you are not winning, you start to get criticized. I went through it when I was here and so did Yzerman in the later years. But all of a sudden they started winning and everything switches. They win the Stanley Cup and he is the hero once again.

The year I was traded, I remember Keith Gave (a hockey writer at the time with the Detroit Free Press) wrote an article in which he quoted one of our players saying that I was more interesting in scoring goals then whether the team wins or loses. I was very hurt by that comment and got into an argument with him after the game. I said that if he was going to put a quote in the paper he should put a player's name beside it. That was a big mistake on my part because the pen is mightier than the sword and he got me big time in the paper a couple of times. It's tough when you are playing for a weak team. My job was to score goals, and I wanted to be the one scoring goals because of that reason. I wasn't a fighter and I wasn't a playmaker, so if I wasn't scoring goals what was I going to do? It doesn't help matters when you are playing on a weak team, end up scoring 50 goals that year and get a very substantial bonus because of it. It definitely created some animosity.

THE TRADE TO QUEBEC

Midway through the 1986-87 season, Ogrodnick was part of a trade with the Quebec Nordiques that sent Brent Ashton, Gilbert Delorme and Mark Krumpel to the Wings in exchange for Ogrodnick, Basil McRae and Doug Shedden. Johnny O was probably most surprised by the move as just weeks before he was assured that he wasn't going to the Nordiques.

The season I was traded to Quebec, Jacques Demers had just taken over the team as head coach. He is definitely a coach that rides on emotion versus being a technical coach. He started to get the team turned around and the Wings enjoyed a few good seasons under his belt. But as time went on there was a mutiny, so to speak, and things really fell apart.

My biggest mistake that year was in training camp. I had gotten hit along side the boards and heard a pop. I had pulled a ligament in my ankle. When the team doctor looked at it he said it wouldn't heal until Christmas time. The injury was quite common with football players. I taped it up from my toe to my shin but there was no tape job that could really support the ankle.

I came back too early. I was really excited to play in the opening game that year and ended up playing only one shift before I had to get off the ice because I couldn't stand on it. A little later on I came back again but I still couldn't turn well. I should have stayed off the ice until it healed because the doctor was right, just around November or December it started feeling strong and the points started coming. I started getting goals and assists. By then it was too late.

In January there was an article in the newspaper saying that I was being traded to Quebec. I was at our morning skate and Jacques Demers came up to me and said, 'John, what's this about you getting traded to Quebec?' I told him I didn't know anything about it. He then told me that he would never trade me to "that Froggie City." Two weeks later I was traded to Quebec.

He (Demers) sometimes says things due to emotion. Maybe he says them before he thinks, but I have also seen it before with other players. Like when Sammy St. Laurent was a goaltender for us. His wife was expecting and we had a meeting in the dressing room talking about various things. Jacques told Sammy not to worry about get sent down to the minors. He said, 'I know your wife is pregnant and that you are worried but you are here to stay.' Same thing, about a week or two later he was down in the minors. He comes across as a very genuine, sincere guy but obviously over time you can see what happens.

We actually played Quebec the night I was traded. Everybody knew it was a six-player deal. That night Doug Shedden, Basil McRae and Peter Klima were not dressed for the game, so everyone in the press box figured it was them. Immediately following the game, I was called into the trainer's room and met with Jacques and Jimmy Devellano (Detroit's

General Manager at the time) and I was told I was just traded to Quebec. I was hurt by it. The only words I could mutter were, 'Jimmy, why Quebec?'

Marc Bergeron (Quebec's head coach) wanted to have two 50-goal scorers on the left side and he already had Michel Goulet. So I finished the season off in Quebec.

It was tough. Quebec City is a very pretty city and has great restaurants, but to live there is a whole different thing. You have the language barrier and the taxes. More importantly we all know that a hockey career doesn't carry much longevity and you have to prepare yourself for life after the game. Another disadvantage was that neither my wife nor daughter could speak French, so it was hard for them as well.

The good thing in Detroit is that you get to know people and get a footing in there for a career after the game. We weren't making a million dollars a year back then playing hockey, so it was tough. I wasn't planning to retire in Quebec. I could have finished off playing the last three or four years of my career in Quebec and then what would I have done?

FINALLY GETTING TO NEW YORK

After only 32 games with the Nordiques, a team that Ogrodnick didn't really want to be traded to in the first place, Johnny O was trying to find a ticket out of Quebec. Sitting out the 1987-88 season training camp, he was hoping for a move somewhere.

I didn't show up for training camp that year and my agent said there could be a deal in the works. As it turned out I had my option of going to the Pittsburgh Penguins or the New York Rangers. At the time the Penguins were offering a first round draft pick. Then (Phil) Esposito found out about it and the Rangers also made an offer. Basically it was our decision and we ended up choosing the Rangers.

New York was a lot of fun after growing up in a small town in Western Canada. We lived in Connecticut and commuted to Madison Square Garden, which was about a 50-mile drive.

Playing there I had an opportunity to talk to certain celebrities and movie stars, which was different and a lot of fun. I remember having a talk with Tim Robbins and Susan Sarandon, it was very interesting.

We had a pretty good team, there is no question about it. We won the Presidents Trophy in the 91-92 season, but the whole time I was there we never made it past the second round of the playoffs.

Our number one line, you could say, was Bernie Nicholls. We also had a pretty good follow-up line with (Kelly) Kisio, (Brian) Mullen and myself. Kisio was injured most of the year so they kept putting Kevin Miller on the line with us. We had quite a bit of success with Miller, but they ended up trading him to Detroit late in the 90-91 season for Joey Kocur.[22] Bottom line was that our line tended to struggle after that. I don't think that we won one game in the last ten games of the season.

Mullen, Kisio and myself had a pretty good year with the Rangers that season. To reward us for our work, the Rangers gave us an open American Express tab. So we went to dinner with our wives to the Rainbow Room, which is a pretty prestigious restaurant on the upper floor of the RCA building. We had a really good time at dinner and ended up ordering a few bottles of their most expensive wine. By the time we finished we had run the bill up more than the Rangers anticipated. At the time all three wives were pregnant, so us three guys were the only ones drinking. My wife started to go into labor while we were at dinner and the following day, she gave birth to our second daughter Breanne. At least I was there for that.

I had fun in New York. I struggled under the Esposito management, but turned it around when Roger Nielson took over. He and Neil Smith gave me an opportunity. Again, a lot of it had to do with the chemistry that we had as a line, which means a lot. Kelly Kisio and Brian Mullen definitely helped me

---

[22] Kevin Miller was part of a trade that also sent Dennis Vial and Jim Cummins to Detroit in exchange for Joe Kocur and Per Djoos heading to the Blueshirts.

out a lot as far as getting my career turned around again and we had a couple of very good years there under Roger Nielson.

My last year in New York, Kisio was taken by San Jose in the expansion draft and Mullen ended up getting traded there for, I think, Tim Kerr. I could feel myself getting phased out. It was very frustrating. At that point I requested to be traded as well, especially if they were not going to use me.

As it turned out, from what Neil Smith was telling me at the time, Minnesota was interested in me because (Brian) Propp had blown out his shoulder. Neil however, was reluctant to give me up for the 3rd or 4th round draft pick that they were offering because he wanted some depth on his team heading into the playoffs in case someone got injured. So he didn't want to give me away for nothing, but at the same time he didn't play me either. It got quite frustrating. I was 33 at the time and it didn't help my career – the end of my career anyway.

BACK TO MOTOWN

After sitting out the remainder of the 91-92 season with New York, Ogrodnick became a free agent in the summer of 1992 and contacted Red Wing management to see about the possibility of playing there once again. Unfortunately for Ogrodnick, it was more of the same back in Detroit. John only played nineteen games that year with the Wings, pushing his decision to retire.

It was tough to find a job as a free agent especially being 33 and not playing much the previous season. I had talked to the Wings' management and they expressed some interest, so I signed a one-year contract with them.

That was kind of frustrating as well. The Wings had a very good team and I didn't expect to play the whole season, but playing in only 19 games was frustrating. At one point they asked me to go down to Adirondack for a few games, so I did. I really didn't like being sent down to the minors as I had played 14 years in the NHL, and got a lot of verbal abuse when I was on the road with them.

When I returned from Adirondack Bryan Murray (Detroit's head coach/general manager at the time) played me seven games in a row and I think I had five goals and a couple of assists, but after that I was out of the line-up. I remember in the playoffs when they were down against Toronto, I hadn't played a game in something like two months and they threw me into the line-up. Obviously, with that big of a layoff, I didn't play that well. The whole season was like that.

Unlike Scotty Bowman, who is not afraid to change the line-up if guys are not giving him 110%, Brian wasn't like that. There were guys that were not playing their best and he would still leave them in. He always made threats to change the line-up but he never did follow through, even though he definitely had the depth in his team to do so. I don't know what Brian's thinking was, or if it was from people up above. People say our fifth line could have played on a top line of a lot of teams in the National Hockey League

I think on the left side he was afraid to break up (Gerard) Gallant with (Steve) Yzerman, and he didn't want to break up (Vyacheslav) Koslov with (Sergei) Federov. Koslov is a very, very good hockey player but at that time I don't think he was quite ready for the NHL.

RETIRED LIFE

Following his 92-93 season with the Red Wings, Ogrodnick made the always-tough

John Ogrodnick continues to reside in the Detroit, Michigan area with wife BettyAnne and daughters KelseyAnne and Breanne. He is self-employed as an investment counselor and remains active in the community as a member of the Red Wing Alumni.

Photo © 1998 Lawrence P. Nader

decision to hang up the skates and move on with his life. Following his career he concentrated becoming an investment counselor, and spent some time with Fox Sports working hockey broadcasts.

The toughest part of hockey is the last season. I played 19 games that year and spent most of my time in the press box. Some of the expansion teams had expressed an interest in me but they ended up bowing out as it got closer to training camp. Then I received a call from John Ferguson, who at the time lived in Windsor and was a scout for Ottawa. He asked me if I was interested in playing for Ottawa. He was very interested, but he went back to Rick Bowness (Ottawa's head coach) who said he wasn't interested at that time. That was basically my last chance.

I took a year off after hockey. Fortunately I had deferred my last contract with the Rangers for six years so I had a steady income during that time. I have always been active in the stock market and I decided to do it professionally. So I went out and got my series 7 license and started working for a large firm in the area which is now called Everen Securities. I worked with them for a couple of years and decided to move off and open up a franchise office. That worked out very well.

I was also doing some work on television with Fox Sports, and that worked out as well. I enjoyed doing that, but I am not interested in doing color or play-by-play. I pretty much had my fill of traveling when I was playing. I'm not interested in being on the road on a consistent basis right now.

Ogrodnick is very happy with where his career and life is heading and does not see himself getting back into the game as a coach. He finally is able to spend time at home and enjoy his family, something that every professional player, and coach for that matter, misses out on during their career.

I have no aspirations to try to get into coaching. I think your first decision after getting out of hockey is to try to stay in the game. I tried that approach, but I am glad that things really didn't work out too well there. I am very happy with what I am doing now. I am able to drive my daughters to school in the morning and I see them during the day. It's worked out really well.

I recently moved my franchise business and am now working out of the house. So I get a chance to see everybody and it works out great.

John, his wife BettyAnne and daughters KelseyAnne (15) and Breanne (9) continue to live in the Detroit Metropolitan area where he also leaves some time in his schedule for play, remaining an active member of the Detroit Red Wing Alumni Association. When his schedule allows, he enjoys strapping the blades back on and getting on the ice in charity competitions. His effort, as well as the efforts of the other Alumni members, is responsible for raising thousands of dollars for various charities and non-profit organizations around Detroit as well as the outlying areas annually.

JOHN OGRODNICK'S CAREER STATS

Season	Team	League	GP	G	A	Pts	PIM
1976-77	New-Westminster Bruins	WHL	14	2	4	6	0
1977-78	New-Westminster Bruins	WHL					
1978-79	New-Westminster Bruins	WHL	72	48	36	84	38
1979-80	Adirondack Red Wings	AHL	39	13	20	33	21
1979-80	Detroit Red Wings	NHL	41	8	24	32	8
1980-81	Detroit Red Wings	NHL	80	35	35	70	14
1981-82	Detroit Red Wings	NHL	80	28	26	54	28
1982-83	Detroit Red Wings	NHL	80	41	44	85	30
1983-84	Detroit Red Wings	NHL	64	42	36	78	14
1984-85	Detroit Red Wings	NHL	79	55	50	105	30
1985-86	Detroit Red Wings	NHL	76	38	32	70	18
1986-87	Detroit Red Wings	NHL	39	12	28	40	6
1986-87	Quebec Nordiques	NHL	32	11	16	27	4
1987-88	New York Rangers	NHL	64	22	32	54	16

JOHN OGRODNICK'S CAREER STATS
(CONT.)

Season	Team	League	GP	G	A	Pts	PIM
1988-89	Denver Rangers	IHL	3	2	0	2	0
1988-89	New York Rangers	NHL	60	13	29	42	14
1989-90	New York Rangers	NHL	80	43	31	74	44
1990-91	New York Rangers	NHL	79	31	23	54	10
1991-92	New York Rangers	NHL	55	17	13	30	22
1992-93	Adirondack Red Wings	AHL	4	2	2	4	0
1992-93	Detroit Red Wings	NHL	19	6	6	12	2
	NHL Totals		**928**	**402**	**425**	**827**	**260**

Pat Peake

NHL Career: 1993-98 (5 seasons)
NHL Teams: Washington Capitals

A hockey players career can be a long successful one, it can be long and mediocre, or it can be short and over before you know it. Pat Peake knows how fast it can all end.

There was a time that "Peaker" had it all in front of him. Staring with the Detroit Compuware Ambassadors of the OHL, who later became the Detroit Jr. Wings (now the Plymouth Whalers), Peake had the makings and talent to become one of the National Hockey League's star players. A series of injuries and illness brought all that crashing down, ending his career after a mere 5 seasons in the NHL.

Over three seasons with the Detroit Ontario Hockey League franchise, the young star played in 162 games scoring 138 goals with 181 assists. After his first season in the OHL, the Washington Capitals selected Peake in the first round (14th overall) of the 1991 NHL Entry Draft. In his first season with the Caps, he scored 29 points (11-17) in 49 games and appeared to be on his way.

Peake, however, spent most of his NHL career either injured or trying to rehab from his injuries. Ironically, while he spent more years in the NHL than he did in the OHL, Peake played only 134 games in The Show.

GROWING UP IN DETROIT

Pat Peake was born and raised in Madison Heights, MI – a suburb of Detroit. It was in his early days that he developed his love for the game of hockey when introduced to it by his father.

My father got me interested in hockey when I was about six years old. He used to play when he was a kid and he, my grandfather and my uncle are all big hockey fans. He took me out skating a few times and it went from there. I really enjoyed it.

I use to watch hockey on TV all the time and wanted to play. I played street hockey constantly, as well.

I started skating in Royal Oak (Michigan) when I was about 6 ½ years old, pushing the chair around on the ice, and started progressing from there. I got on a few house teams there and then moved on to play for the Compuware and Little Caesers programs. It was something I took to. My dad asked if I liked the sport and said, 'If it's something you want to do, do it. We'll help you on your way.' I loved the game since day one.

Peake never saw himself as anything more than one of the average players on a team until he started playing at the Pee Wee level.

I played Squirt major, I was triple 'A' and we went on to win some tournaments. I was just one of the average players on the team. I didn't progress any better than the other players until I was about Pee Wee.

Pee Wee minor and Pee Wee major I played for Art Van. Our coach was Bob Petrie. We kind of had the same group together for a few years and we had some dynamite teams. We'd win the league every year and go on all these tournaments. That's when I really started to step up a little bit. I won several MVP awards in the tournaments. We played in five tournaments and I ended up winning five MVP awards. It was something I wanted to do and was having the greatest time at it.

I played baseball then too. There came a point when I started playing Tier II hockey and Federation Baseball at the same time, that I had to make a decision on what I wanted to play. This was after we went to the Quebec tournament as Pee Wees and several tournaments from Bantam. I was about 15.

When I stepped up to Tier II I was playing in the Compuware system for Andy Wiedenbach. That was when I realized that I had a chance to make a career of playing. It was something I did because I loved the game and it was fun for me. My parents were very supportive.

THE ONTARIO HOCKEY LEAGUE YEARS

"Peaker" played for Compuware in the Tier II system in the North American Hockey League before being selected by Compuware's newly formed Ontario Hockey League franchise – the Detroit Ambassadors – in the 1990-91 season. Playing for the Ambassadors was the ideal situation for Peake, as it allowed him to follow his dream of advancing to the NHL while being able to finish school at home.

I skipped midget hockey and played Bantam major. After that I was approached by Andy Wiedenbach who was coaching the Tier II team for Compuware. We had a great team there. The three centers on our team were (Eric) Lindros, (Brian) Rolston, and myself. We all went in the top 14 of the 1991 NHL draft, which is pretty amazing.

Eric left the team just after Christmas to go play for Oshawa in the OHL. But that was a great season. We had a lot of great players on the team – Andrew Shyer and Jim Storm were my wingers. I had a great year and really progressed.

I knew that Compuware was getting an OHL team and they were interested in me. It was a perfect situation for me to be able to finish at the high school I went to and still play in the OHL. It was a big decision because University of Michigan and Michigan State University also approached me, so it was a tough decision for me to make. I went and visited a few of the schools, but the key was that I wanted to get to the NHL the fastest way possible. That was my goal. So I had to make a decision and luckily the Ambassadors drafted me first overall their first year.

The first year with the Ambassadors was real tough. I think we won 11 games that year out of 66. We went through some growing pains that season.

Then we moved over to play our games at Joe Louis instead of Cobo Arena the next year and the team started to progress. We got some good draft picks and made some good trades.

My last year there I was playing with Kevin Brown and Bob Wren as my linemates. They were both outstanding players. They had great hands, great skills and great heads for the game. I also played the point with Todd Harvey and Blair Scott. That was our five-man power play. I don't remember our percentage, but it was dynamite.

I put up some good numbers that year and broke the record for the fastest 50 goals in OHL history, doing it in 33 games. I look back at it and it was a team effort. The game was so much fun; it was easy. We went out there and we knew we were going to be successful. We knew where each other were going to be on the ice.

Coming back from pro camp helped me a lot, too. I was drafted in 1991. The year that I did so well was the 92-93 season, when I put up 136 points (58-78) and won CHL Player of the Year. But at that point I had been through two pro camps and had signed a contract. I knew what direction I was headed in and what part of the game I had to work on. I was just having a lot of fun.

PLAYING PRO

Following his first year in the OHL, Peake went to the NHL Entry Draft knowing that he would be selected, but unsure of where he would go. Several teams had shown interest, but scouting reports varied on his position in the draft.

I remember my draft day real clearly. I was rated 8th in one scouting report and 15th on another. You just have no idea where you are going to go at. I was at The Aud in Buffalo, my family was there with me. It was just the greatest feeling. You sit there on the edge of your seat. We knew the first couple of picks, but after that it was up for grabs.

I thought maybe I was going to Dallas (Minnesota at the time), they had showed quit a bit of interest in me. They ended up taking (Richard) Matvichuk that year. I also thought maybe I'd go to New Jersey, who picked 11th. It was just a great thrill. To go in the top 14 is a great honor. You're sitting on the edge of your seat as each team goes up to the podium because you really don't know who's going to take you. It's an very exciting and a great, great day.

Peake was eventually selected 14th overall by the Washington Capitals – the team that he would play for his whole, albeit short, career.

The first year I went up and played a few games for Baltimore, who was Washington's minor league team that year. I missed a few games of the OHL season that year and was sent back to the Jr. Wings because at my age group I still had junior eligibility remaining and I couldn't stay in the minors. I had to be sent back to my OHL team. That was the year I put up the great numbers.

I finished that season out with the Detroit Junior Wings and broke my ankle – the one that is now my good ankle – against Guelph in game 2 of the playoffs. The team went on to win a couple of rounds, but unfortunately it wasn't enough. I won the Canadian Hockey League's Player of the Year Award that year, but the Soo (Sault Ste. Marie Greyhounds) won the Memorial Cup.

After that season I went to live in Washington for the summer and trained with their training coach. I planned to step in and make the team. I had a real good training camp. Washington had a real good season the year before. I think that was their record setting season. The team was pretty stacked. So I started the season in Portland – their minor league team.

I played four games in Portland, never scoring a goal. Washington, however, started 0-6 that year and they quickly brought up three guys to make changes. Along with myself, they brought up John Slaney and Decon Walcheck. I remember my first three games clearly.

My first game was against Buffalo. They had Pat Lafontaine and Grant Fuhr at the time. Lafontaine was one of my idols growing up. I use to watch him when he was playing junior for Compuware. He was a great, great player. The second game was against Pittsburgh with Mario Lemieux, and my third game was against Los Angeles and Wayne Gretzky.

I stepped in the right way. The first three games were quite memorable and things went from there. I played 49 games that year and had some injuries. I was playing on the third and fourth line, but was learning a lot. We had a strong team and it was a tough line to crack. Playing on the third and fourth line you don't see as much ice as you'd like, but I got my feet wet and went from there.

The first game against Buffalo, I played well and ended up having seven shots on net. The second game I got my first point, which was an assist. Then we beat L.A., and I ended up getting three assists that game. So here I am, a 20-year-old hot dog playing against the three best players and I had four points in three games.

I took three penalties in the game against the Kings, and all three happened to be against Gretzky. You know, if you touched him you got a penalty. But I didn't know whether to bump into the guy or what. I am all on adrenaline, playing against Wayne Gretzky. Obviously you can't let him go, but you don't want to hit him because you want him to sign your jersey after the game.

It was just a great thrill playing against those guys. You just kind of pinch yourself, you're in awe. A year ago you were in the OHL, sitting on the bus for 10 hours, and now here you are in the NHL playing against Mario Lemieux, Wayne Gretzky and your boyhood idol Pat Lafontaine. It was a great feeling.

The following year was the lockout year and I came down with mono. I only played a few games that season. I had played center my whole career, but when I went to Washington they wanted me to play wing. It was new for me. As a winger in the NHL, you get the puck along the boards and if you don't know right away what you are going to do with it, you are going to pay.

The lockout lasted until January and then I was diagnosed with mononucleosis. I had played about 15 or 16 games with Washington and they were asking what was going on with me. I wasn't performing, I wasn't playing like I should have been playing. They said, 'In training camp you were our best player. What happened?' Finally they said, 'If you don't get your act together, we are going to send you down for a little while.'

So I went to the doctor and they did some blood work because I just wasn't feeling right. The next day I came in and they said they were going to send me to Portland to play four games in four nights. They wanted me to score some goals and get my confidence back. As soon as I got into Portland, there was a call for me at the airport. They wanted me to head back to Washington because the tests showed that I had mono. I had been playing with it for those 16 games.

They told me to go home and get to bed. They said to stay home until I saw the doctor again in a few weeks. That answered a lot of questions about why I felt like I was skating with a piano on my back.

THE INJURY BUG

Just when things were starting to look like Peake would break through that barrier and solidify his position in the NHL, he was hit by a freak career-ending injury. Many times we focus on the long, flourishing careers that players have in the NHL, however there is another side. A side that Pat Peake now knows all too well. Sometimes it doesn't mater how good you could be, careers are cut short due to injury.

The year I hurt myself was the year that I really started to go. I played 62 games and scored 17 goals and 19 assists. Twelve of my 17 goals came on the power play and some were game winners. Things were really starting to pick up. I was playing more in a productive role. I was on the ice in the last few minutes of the game, playing against the other team's top two lines. The coach was showing a lot of confidence in me and things were really going well.

We got into the playoffs and I had a couple of goals against Pittsburgh, again on the power play and was playing very well. I had a total of four or five points in the playoffs. Then in game 5, I was racing for an icing and before you know it it's over.

I was chasing J.J Daigneault and, I gave him a hook about the bottom of the circle to try to beat him. It was in the second period of an emotional game. I went to kick the puck and as I did we both kind of fell. My skate blade had gotten caught where the boards and the ice meet. I rolled over and, as soon as I did, I knew something was wrong.

Peake summed it all up by saying his career ending injury was mentally hell. No one wakes up each morning and thinks that their career could end that day, especially at age 24 with the whole world in front of you. The bitter reality is that it is a tough sport and at any minute, your career can come to an end. Even after the physical pain is gone, the player has to deal with the mental anguish of it all being over.

I finally just watched the video after three years. It was very hard to watch. It's something I just have to deal with. It's harder mentally than it is physically. The older guys, that have retired, played and they know how good they were. I will never know how good I could have been. That's something that eats at me every day. I was improving each day. Could I have been a 40-goal scorer? There are so many unanswered questions.

As a hockey player, you expect to have two careers, you can only play for so long. But nobody expected that at age 24, I would start my new career that early. It's something you work at your whole life to achieve, then just like that it's taken from you. Mentally it has been hell, to say the least.

CAREER'S END

Pat's heel shattered that day into numerous pieces. The doctors said that it was an injury they have never seen happen to a hockey player. It was an injury that happens to people who are in car accidents and construction workers that fall from heights and land on their heel. It had never happened to a hockey player before.

You first reaction when your get the news from your doctor, is that you think he is lying. You want to just grab him, choke him to death and tell him he's lying. I've done this my whole life. You want to tell him, 'They can do triple bypasses when people have heart attacks, they implant fake organs, why can't you fix my foot.'

Here it is three years and seven surgeries later and it's still not right. When the heel shatters like that, it is like an egg. It actually broke in nine or ten places. They had to put it back together like a puzzle, using 12 screws and a plate.

I finally got those out, and now half of my foot is numb because they removed a nerve.

The first surgery was to repair it. The next surgery they wanted to fuse the joint allowing me motion only up and down. If they did that there would be no way that I could ever play hockey again, or even walk on a hillside. I said that there had to be another way.

I've been through seven surgeries total, to date, and had countless cortisone shots. I'd come back, skate a bit, and things would be going all right. Then I would go into the doctor and he'd do another MRI and find something else was torn. He took a nerve out, removed a small bone to allow more room, cleaned the joint, and put a groove in the joint so the tendon would slide better.

I have had great doctors and I have improved a lot over the last couple of surgeries. Now it's into the tendon, which has been torn so many times that one day it's good the next day it's bad. I also have arthritis in the joint. There comes a time that you have to say, 'Life goes on after hockey.' I want to be able to walk my kids through the park in 10-15 years.

BEST MEMORIES

Every player that has ever laced up the skates, and taken the ice, has their favorite memories of the game. Pat Peake is no exception. Through all the heartache, there were a lot of memorable events.

Winning the Canadian Hockey League Player of the Year was a great honor. That was something that was spawned by a great team and great coaching staff. It was one of the best things I remember.

Getting drafted into the NHL by Washington is as clear as yesterday. What a thrill it was to be picked number 14 overall.

Playing those first three games, that I spoke about earlier, against some of the superstars in the league also ranks up there. Also scoring my first goal.

It took me 11 games to notch that first one. It was in Pittsburgh against Tom Barrasso, who will be a Hall of Fame goaltender. To score my first NHL goal on him was a thrill. I still have that puck on the wall. The team mounted it nicely on a plaque for me with the date and the goalie's name. It's a great memory. It's something I can look at every day and be proud of.

WORDS OF WISDOM

Hockey is a game played by children and adults alike, with youthful enthusiasm and vigor. It is a game, but it can also be dangerous. Careers are ended in injury all the time, and in rare cases, worse. For those of you who play the game, young and old, Pat has some words of wisdom.

I think Wayne Gretzky said it very well when he retired. He said, 'Cherish every moment. Play the game because you love the game, not because you are going to make a lot of money and become famous.' All that's going to come in time.

You should play the game strictly because you love the game. That would be my advice to young kids today. Play it as hard as you can every day. Make the most of every time on the ice, because you never know when it's going to be your last.

PAT PEAKE'S CAREER STATS

Season	Team	League	GP	G	A	Pts	PIM
1990-91	Detroit Ambassadors	OHL	63	39	51	90	54
1991-92	Detroit Ambassadors	OHL	53	41	52	93	44
1991-92	Baltimore Skipjacks	AHL	3	1	0	1	4
1992-93	Detroit Jr. Wings	OHL	46	58	78	136	64
1993-94	Portland Pirates	AHL	4	0	5	5	2
1993-94	Washington Capitals	NHL	49	11	18	29	39
1994-95	Portland Pirates	AHL	5	1	3	4	2
1994-95	Washington Capitals	NHL	18	0	4	4	12
1995-96	Washington Capitals	NHL	62	17	19	36	46
1996-97	Portland Pirates	AHL	3	0	2	2	0
1996-97	Washington Capitals	NHL	4	0	0	0	4
1997-98	Washington Capitals	NHL	1	0	0	0	4
	NHL Totals		**134**	**28**	**41**	**69**	**105**

Jimmy Peters, Sr.

NHL Career: 1945-54 (9 seasons)
NHL Teams: Montreal Canadiens. Boston Bruins, Detroit Red Wings, Chicago Blackhawks

In his nine NHL seasons, Jimmy Peters, Sr. played in 574 regular-season NHL games scoring 125 goals with 150 assists, while acquiring 186 penalty minutes. He also played in 60 playoff games netting 5 goals and 9 assists. Peters had the dubious honor of having his name engraved on three Stanley Cups, an average of one championship team every three years. His first Stanley Cup was with the 1945-46 Montreal Canadiens, while the other two came with the 1949-50 and 1953-54 Detroit Red Wings.

Peters was born in 1922 and like many hockey players in the 1940's saw his playing career interrupted by World War II.[23] Upon returning from his tour of duty, Peters was greeted at the train station by the Montreal Canadiens, who had secured his rights, and told he was playing that same night. He was taken from the station to the arena and his NHL career began.

YOUNGER DAYS

I'm from Montreal. When I was a kid growing up I was really a hockey fanatic. I played my youth hockey there. Back

---

[23] During World War II, many Canadien players were called home to join the Canadian Armed Forces in the fight in Europe, prompting depletion of NHL team rosters. Many of the World's best players at that time were playing for Canadien Armed Forces teams in both Canada and Europe. The war and huge debts forced NHL's New York Americans team to fold in 1942.

in those days, we didn't have mini-mites or mites, it was strictly Bantam, Midget, Juvenile, Junior, Senior, Professional and Major League hockey.

When I was 18 I went to play for the Oshawa Generals in Ontario. Oshawa was a big-name team then. I went there and got a job for the summer prior to the start of hockey season in the fall. However, before I could begin my season with Oshawa, I was drafted by the New York Americans and never played with the Generals.

From there, I went to the New York American's training camp and turned pro in 1941. That was the start of my history as a player in the National Hockey League."

I went to the American's training camp and was farmed out to the Springfield Indians, which was New York's American Hockey League farm team at the time. When the Americans sent me down, they told me I'd be back on Friday, but they forgot to tell me what year.

The American League back then was pretty well on level with the National Hockey League. They had a lot of great hockey players. I finished that year in Springfield. We made it to the playoffs and were beat out by Cleveland. After that I came home and joined the army."

I played a little bit of hockey in the Army before being shipped overseas. We were playing an exhibition game, in Kingston, Ontario, against the Detroit Red Wings, who had Red Kelly, Ted Lindsay, Gordie Howe and Harry Lumley at the time, when Jack Adams (Detroit's General Manager) came up to me and asked how I'd like to play for Detroit? I said that it would be nice, and that was all I said. Years later when I was traded from Boston to Detroit, Mr. Adams said to me, 'See son, I told you I'd get you.'

LES CANADIENS

While it was the dream of most every Canadian youngster, back then, to grow up to play professional hockey for Les Habs, Peters was quite surprised to have that honor thrust upon him upon his return from World War II. While he never became a superstar during his playing days, he was a solid contributor that played for three Stanley Cup Champions during his nine-year career.

I got married before returning home to join the Army, and while I was overseas in the military my wife gave birth to twins, a boy and a girl. When I came back in October of 1945, I found out that the Montreal Canadiens had drafted me.

I was returning from overseas when Dirk Irvin and several newspaper men met me at the railroad station. They said that I was playing for the Canadiens. I hadn't even seen my wife or my children yet and they wanted me to go and skate in the Forum that day.

I told them that I had a wife and two children I had never seen and that I just wanted to get a job and take care of my family. My wife was in New Brunswick, which is where she is from, with our children at her parents home. They said, 'No. You are playing for Montreal.'

That afternoon I went down to the Forum and skated. A few days later my wife and children came to Montreal, and a week later I signed a contract with the Canadiens."

We had six teams then. Each team only had 15 players. There was always an odd man out, looking over your shoulder. If you made a few mistakes, you'd be pulling splinters (sitting the bench). I was fortunate to come back from the service, play for Montreal and win a Stanley Cup my first year there (1945-46).

"I played in Montreal with guys like Rocket Richard, who I had played junior with. When we were in juniors we were on the third line and didn't play very much. The following year, Richard got up to senior hockey and broke an ankle. The following year he turned pro and broke a wrist. The next year, he scored 50 goals.

We had a lot of great players. Fellows like Toe Blake. I thought the guy was just a winner and a great person. I thought the world of Toe Blake. Then there was Bill Durnam, Rocket Richard and Elmer Lach. They kind of took me under their wing.

You can't realize how exciting it is to win a Stanley Cup. The poor fan out there gets excited, but just think of the player that has never been on a Stanley Cup team. It's just the greatest thing. You think you own the world. Of course that wears off and you have to go back to work again.

But winning the Stanley Cup for the first time is the greatest thing for any hockey player. That is the ultimate in life."

The Canadiens played for the Cup that year against Boston, downing the Bruins 4 games to 1. In one of the games, in overtime, Peters scored the winning goal, but never saw it.

My linemates were Billy Reay and Murph Chamberlain, and we checked the Kraut line of (Bobby) Bauer, (Milt) Schmidt and (Woody) Dumart. We were just making a line change when I got the puck and made a backhand shot into the end of the rink. I turned to head to the bench and the next thing I knew there was a bunch of guys on top of me. They told me I scored the goal, but I don't know what happened. I never saw it.

LIFE AFTER MONTREAL

Jimmy's stay in Montreal was shot but sweet. Midway though his third season as a Canadien, Peters was packed off to Beantown in a deal that sent two players to Montreal. After a year and a half with Boston, Peters was traded to Detroit before being sent to Chicago and then returning to Detroit to finish his career.

In 1947 Montreal traded me to Boston. I was the most surprised guy. Frank Selke told me that they didn't want to trade me, but Rocket Richard was hurt at that particular time and they weren't getting any scoring. Montreal got Joe Carveth and another player in the deal.

I played for the Bruins for 1 ½ seasons before being traded to the Detroit Red Wings in 1949. It seemed strange that no one wanted me, but everyone wanted me.

I remember playing for the Detroit Red Wings and facing the Chicago Blackhawks. The first game was at Olympia. James Norris Sr. (Detroit's owner) came to the dressing room and told us, "Boys, if there was ever a hockey team I want you to beat it's those Blackhawks." Boy did we get fired up. Then they traded me to Chicago and we were getting ready for a game against Detroit and the same guy comes to our dressing room and gives us the same speech. I said to myself, 'What the hell is going on here.' We never knew they [the Norris family] owned both teams. As players were so gullible that we didn't know these things.

At the start of the 1951-52 season, Adams said for me to go to Chicago and that I would back in Detroit by Christmas. So I agreed. Sid Abel was coaching Chicago then. When Mr. Adams tried to get me back, Sid said I was doing well in Chicago and he wanted to keep me there. I didn't return to Detroit until late in the 53-54 season.

We had some good teams when I was in Detroit, and they always treated me well. I enjoyed my stay in Detroit so much, that after I retired from hockey, got a job and stayed here.

SOME OF THE BEST

During his nine years in the NHL, Peters played with, and against, some greatest names in the sport. While he was never selected to the Hockey Hall of Fame, a great number of his teammates, from the three Stanley Cup teams he played on, were inducted. Peters offers us his thought on a few of these players.

Going back to the six teams, every team had a big line. For instance, Montreal had the Punch Line with Elmer Lach, Maurice Richard and Toe Blake. Boston had the Kraut Line with Woody Dumont, Milt Schmidt and Bobby Bauer. Chicago had the Pony Line with brothers Doug and Max Bentley and Bill Mosienko. Toronto was always a thorn in your side. But everybody had a variety of good hockey players. Of course there were probably only two Americans in the league then. The players were almost all Canadian.

I think the greatest little hockey player in the world was Ted Lindsay. Sure he played with Gordie Howe, and maybe a lot of guys would have been better hockey players if they were lined with Howe, but Lindsay was great on his own. I remember playing one night with Lindsay and Howe, I jumped over the boards, only took about two steps and passed the puck and got an assist. That's how good they were on the ice.

When Rocket Richard touched the puck, his eyes were just fire. I was watching TV a few weeks ago and they were showing clips of Richard. You could still see the fire in his eyes. Every time he took a shot it was on the net. When I was playing, my wife used to ask me how come when I took a shot on the net I would miss the net. She'd ask, 'How do you do that when you're shooting at the net.'

Ted Kennedy, from the Toronto Maple Leafs, was one guy that at first I didn't think could skate, shoot, or score. He turned out to be a very good player. As an individual, I thought he was outstanding. He was on power plays, he was their leader, and he was everything. I talked to Joe Klukay about him and Joe agrees. I thought he was great.

But, if I were to pick my all-time great hockey players, based on whom I played against and with, the fellows I would pick in goal are Terry Sawchuck and Bill Durnam. On defense I would have to say Bill Gadsby and Doug Harvey. On forward, I would take Gordie Howe, Rocket Richard and Ted Lindsay, play them in any position you want and I think I would have the best in the world.

However, there is a fellow that has come along by the name of Gretzky who I think has done a super, super job with the game of hockey.

TODAY'S SALARIES

When Peters began playing in the National Hockey League, if you earned $5,000 a year, you were doing well. Today salaries have surpassed the multi-million dollar mark in US currency for average players, not to mention what players like (Eric) Lindros, (Pavel) Bure, (Jaromir) Jagr and (Sergei)

Fedorov command. The salary escalator has Peters concerned for the future of the game.

You have to look at these salaries that the players are making today and wonder where does it end? The poor fan, the ordinary guy going to work, can't afford to take his kid to a game.

They [the teams] carry 21 or 22 players and say, just for the sake of argument, one guy is making $35 million for five years. How do the rest of these guys respond to that? I think that the guy that is making the $35 million for five years should be putting on the red light to win the games. They're paying him enough.

When we were younger, we didn't know any better. We had never even heard of an agent. For us to make $5,000 was something. Back then, to go to work and make $5,000 a year was something you just couldn't do, unless you had a supervisor or managers job.

Then the agents came along. I think they are the guys creating the problems. They are making big bucks off of it as well. I mean how much do you need?

ALMOST A REF

Following his time playing the game, Peters entered the officiating ranks for college and senior hockey. At one point the NHL decided it was best to approach retired players to become referees in the league, determining no one was better to call the game then a guy who had been there. Many were asked, some accepted, and yet others, like Peters, declined the offer figuring the potential downside was not worth it.

When I got out of hockey, I got into a refereeing a little bit of college and senior hockey. One day I got a phone call from Jack Adams, he wanted me to have lunch in downtown Detroit with him, Frank Selke and Carl Voss, who was the referee in chief for the NHL. We had lunch and went up to their suite to continue talking. They asked me what would I think about becoming an official.

I said that I was proud that they thought about Jimmy Peters but was there anyone else that they had approached? They said they had approached Bob Goldham, Gaye Stewart and myself. I was told that Goldham had turned the job down and Stewart had taken it.

I asked Frank Selke what would happen if I was refereeing in Montreal and made a mistake? He said that they would forgive me. I then said, "what if I make another mistake." When he hesitated. I said, "in that case I don't want the job." Gaye Stewart refereed one game and was gone.

Later, I was lying on the couch at home one Sunday morning and I got a phone call. They asked me if I would fill in to be a linesman in a game that night at Olympia. I said sure. I get down there and Matt Pavelich is the referee. It was his first game as a referee. Matt had always been a good linesman.

The game was going along pretty well. Toronto had scored a couple of goals. Then at the end of the second period, there

Jimmy Peters, Sr. passed on an offer by Frank Selke and Carl Voss to become a referee in the National Hockey League and never regretted his decision. Today, at age 79, he continues to keep himself young by filling that exact role during Red Wing Alumni charity games.

Photo © 1998 Lawrence P. Nader

was a bang on the door of the officials' room and in comes Jack Adams. He rips that poor Matt Pavelich from one end to the other. Carl Voss was sitting there and hadn't opened his mouth at all. After Adams walked out I told Voss that I was sure glad that I didn't accept the job when they offered it to me if that was the way he was going to be my boss. Matt Pavelich never refereed another game. Matt went back to being a linesman and stayed there until he retired from the NHL.

That's how strong those guys [like Adams] were in the league.

JIMMY THE COACH

After joining the work force and establishing himself with a regular day job, Peters accepted an offer to begin coaching the Detroit Jr. Wings in the evenings.

When they started the Junior Red Wings, I was asked to come down and coach the team. I just needed to teach them the basics. I was working a day job at the time, but I use to be down at the Olympia six nights a week.

In my conversations with Mr. Adams, I told him that I believed that the American boy, given the ice time, could become a good hockey player. That was when I began to get the ice any time it was available. We'd be down there five nights a week or more for practice.

When we started the team, we placed an ad in the paper asking for anyone who could skate or shoot a puck to come down to the Olympia for a try-out. To my surprise, we probably had 300 kids show up. In order to break things down, I took about 20 kids at a time and had them skate up and down the rink as fast as they could. I would pick out the guys that could skate and move on to the next group.

From there the team grew.

After gaining success with the Jr. Wings, Peters was approached by the Red Wings about coaching their farm club in Memphis of the Central Hockey League.

It was the last game of the season (with Memphis), and we needed a tie or a win to get into the playoffs. We were playing against Omaha, who were the New York Rangers farm club. They were the best team in the Central League at that time.

To make a long story short, we were leading 2-1 with about two minutes remaining in the game, when we got a penalty. I wasn't worried about playing a man short because we had a pretty good penalty-killing unit. Then with about 40 seconds to go, we get another penalty. We are now two men short and they had the best power play in the league. I knew I had to be inventive to win the game.

Before the face-off I tapped one of the players on the shoulder and told him that as soon as Omaha got possession of the puck, he was to jump on the ice. The players thought I had lost my mind.

So they dropped the puck and the play went around and, when Omaha got possession of the puck, my player jumped on the ice. The referee blew the whistle and we had another penalty, but 15 seconds had ticked off the clock.

Before the next face-off I, once again, instructed another player to jump on the ice as soon as Omaha got possession of the puck. He did and they blew the whistle again. I am now missing four players, but I could not be down more than two players on the ice on the ice anyway. Meanwhile another 20 seconds had gone by.

At this point the referee came over to me and said, 'You know you are going to fill up the penalty box?' I told him I wasn't worried about that because we would win the game 2-1 and that gets us in the playoffs.

We won the game and that night I phoned Sid Abel, who was the general manager of Memphis, and told him he was going to get some repercussion from what I did. He said, 'Good for you Shaky (Peters nickname).'

As a result, the next year the rule was changed and, I believe, the other team would be awarded a penalty shot if you did that today.

STILL SKATING AFTER ALL THESE YEARS

Today, Jimmy Peters remains extremely active in both the business and hockey ends of life. Peters continues to work sales for an automation machine company in the Detroit area, as well as actively participate with the Detroit Red Wing Alumni.

Peters, until 1996, still skated in each of the Alumni charity games as a player, but has since moved to the referee's position. The organization plays numerous charity games during the hockey season and Jimmy can be seen refereeing at every one. Always one to love the ice, he even continues skating while the zamboni resurfaces, leaving the rink only once the game is over.

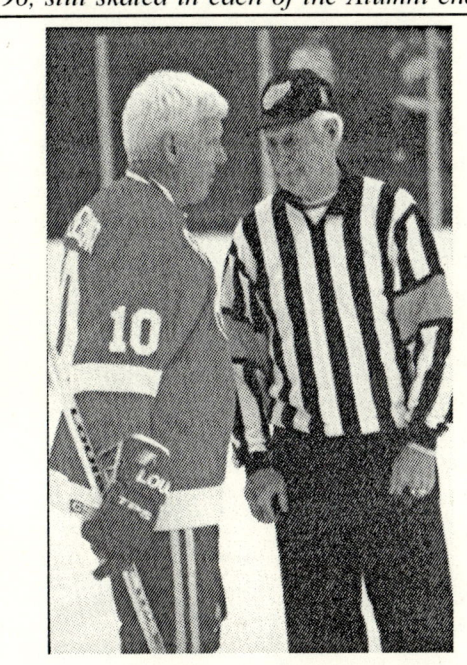

Jimmy Peters, Sr. takes a moment to chat with NHL great Alex Delvecchio during a charity event in 1998.
Photo © 1997 Lawrence P. Nader

It is the camaraderie, more then the physical aspects of the Alumni's games, that keeps Peters going. Swapping stories with other players his era and younger, as well as knowing that you are helping others less fortunate, is closer to the fountain of youth then most people will ever come.

We are a very active group of hockey players and we love to help raise money for a lot of different charities. I have a lot of fun at it and it keeps me young.

JIMMY PETER, SR.'S CAREER STATS

Season	Team	League	GP	G	A	Pts	PIM
1941-42	Philadelphia	AHL	0	0	0	0	0
1941-42	Springfield	AHL		12	18	30	10
1945-46	Montreal Canadiens	NHL	47	11	19	30	10
1946-47	Montreal Canadiens	NHL	60	11	13	24	27
1947-48	Montreal Canadiens	NHL	22	1	3	4	6
1947-48	Boston Bruins	NHL	37	12	15	27	38
1948-49	Boston Bruins	NHL	60	16	15	31	8
1949-50	Detroit Red Wings	NHL	70	14	16	30	20
1950-51	Detroit Red Wings	NHL	68	17	21	38	14
1951-52	Chicago Blackhawks	NHL	70	15	21	36	16
1952-53	Chicago Blackhawks	NHL	69	22	19	41	16
1953-54	Chicago Blackhawks	NHL	46	6	4	10	21
1953-54	Detroit Red Wings	NHL	25	0	4	4	10
1954-55	Windsor	OHAS	46	25	31	56	0
1955-56	Windsor	OHAS	48	12	37	49	0
NHL Totals			**574**	**125**	**150**	**275**	**186**

Wayne Presley

NHL Career: 1984-96 (14 seasons)
NHL Teams: Chicago Blackhawks, San Jose Sharks, Buffalo Sabres, Toronto Maple Leafs

Throughout his career, Wayne Presley was known as an antagonizer, an instigator if you will. He had a way to get under the opposition's skin, taking their focus off the game at hand, and many times drawing his opponent into a penalty. According to Presley, this talent came naturally.

Through his 14 seasons in the NHL, "Elvis" as he was called by teammates, played for five different teams before retiring from the game. While he came close to winning the Stanley Cup with Chicago, it was not to be. His championship cup realization did come true, though, after he retired from the NHL.

Returning to his home in the Detroit, Michigan area, Presley decided to give the IHL a shot when he was called by the Detroit Vipers. The Vipers were looking for help in solidifying their chances of winning the Turner Cup and Presley wanted a shot at capturing the chalice. The mixture was perfect as both Presley and the Vipers took home the Turner Cup that season in 1997.

EARLY DAYS IN THE GAME

Presley remembers when he started playing hockey, in Taylor, Michigan, as a youth. He remembers his first season being on an outside rink and the freezing cold. What he doesn't know is why he got into the game.

Everyone asks me why I got into hockey. I really don't know why my parents put me in hockey, because they never really watched it or anything. My grandfather watched it. He grew up in Dresden, Ontario, so maybe that's why.

I started playing and I liked it. I played on an outdoor rink my first year. It's hard to remember, going back to when you were a kid. I remember being cold, my toes freezing. My mom always said 'You never quit.' She asked a couple of times and I always said I didn't want to quit. I don't remember that, but I remember the freezing and all the bad stuff.

It was good playing there in Taylor. It was just a city team, but I had a lot of fun. I was one of the best players. My whole career, it seemed like I never knew I could do anything until I got there. I never knew I could make AAA, I never knew I could go to juniors, I never knew I could make the pros, until I started playing against players of that caliber. I don't know if I was underestimating myself. I just didn't realize it could happen to me.

I played with Little Caesars[24] my whole minor hockey career. I start with them in squirts. The first year I played for Mr. Ilitch, we had a lot of good players on the team. Like I said, until you get there you don't know that you can play with these kids. I went out and made the team, and as it turned out we made the State Championship my first year playing for them. That was pretty cool.

I guess that got my foot in the door. I played my whole minor career in their system. We won the State Championship five times. Finally the last year, in Midgets, we won the National Championship. So every year I got there.

Then I got to the point that I was looking at junior players. The Guys that went to junior and made it, played well. So when the next step came, the Kitchener Rangers (OHL) drafted me in the seventh round. I went up there and it amazed me. I wasn't the best player there, but I was holding my own.

---

[24] Detroit Red Wings' Owner Mike Ilitch also owns a chain of pizzerias called Little Caesers. This business also sponsors numerous youth teams in Michigan playing at various levels of minor hockey.

THE ONTARIO HOCKEY LEAGUE

I played pretty well my first year with Kitchener, then I was drafted by Chicago[25] after that. After I played my first year with Kitchener, I realized that I had a chance of turning pro. My first year at training camp there was Al McInnis, Scott Stevens, Brian Bellows, Wendell Young, Dave Shaw, John Tucker, and Mike Eagles. All these guys played in the NHL. I was playing with them and I was keeping up. That's when I realized that I had a shot at it.

All the people asked, "You're not going to college?" I had a couple of offers, but back then you couldn't commit to anybody, and they couldn't commit to you, until your senior year. You have to decide before that to go to juniors. I forfeited my college eligibility and said, "Start paying me my $100 a week, I want to play junior." Everybody thought I was crazy, but after that first week in September, I knew I would be all right. I didn't know that I was going to make it to the NHL but I knew I would get drafted pretty high and I would have a crack at it.

Now that the rules have changed (concerning eligibility), I probably would have went and played at Michigan or somewhere. If I could have played college hockey and realized, like it is now, that I could have made it to the NHL, that's probably what I would have done. That's what I am telling my kid to go, go to school and have a good time. Even if you don't make it to the NHL, you're going to be somebody there. Go to a campus that loves hockey.

I wish they had changed the rules back in my day where I could have gotten a good education out of it as well. The way it is now, if you're going to make, you're going to make it.

So I had a pretty good rookie year (39 goals and 48 assists), but the really big year was the next year (63g-76a). In that year, I broke Dwight Foster's record up there. That's when I really knew I could make it, as I was probably one of the best players in the league. We went to the Memorial Cup my second year.

---

[25] Presley was selected with Chicago's second round pick (39th overall) in the 1983 NHL Entry Draft.

That was really big. The National Championship was big, but nowhere near as big as what Canada has.

I was traded to the Soo (Sault Ste. Marie) for my last two months in junior and we went to the Memorial Cup again, but we didn't win. Then I turned pro.

TURNING PRO

Turning pro is rarely easy and usually requires a player spending some time in the minor leagues. Presley made the transaction from juniors to the NHL easier than most. After being sent to the American Hockey League by the Blackhawks to start the 1985-86 season, the young right winger returned to the Windy City after only 29 games in the minor leagues.

When I turned pro with Chicago, they had a decent team, but I wouldn't say that they were great. They sent me down to Halifax for a couple of months (Nova Scotia in the AHL). I don't know if I was over-confident at that time or what, but they sent me back. Nova Scotia's team was split between Chicago players and Edmonton players. Our coach, Larry Kisch, hated all the Chicago players, except me.

He said, 'I'm going to send you up to sample the big league and maybe you'll come back down and really turn it on.' Once he sent me up there I never came back. Everybody has to have a break in their career somewhere, and I think that was my break.

I was just an average player that played pretty well, and if I would have kept going the way I was, I don't know how long I would have been there. Then (Mike) Keenan came along, and he really hated me.

To him I was average until the playoffs. I had two good playoffs in a row. We went to the final four two years in a row. They went to the cup the year they traded me. But I think those two years really made my career. People looked at me and said, 'We really want a player to help out in the playoffs,' so they traded for me.

Going from not making it the first year to playing good in the playoffs for two years in a row and losing out to the Stanley Cup Champions, I thought that made my career.

In 1987 I played on the Canada Cup team. I don't know how I got there. It had to be politics, because Bob Pulford really liked me and he was the General Manager of the team. I scored 32 goals that year so I had some decent numbers. The guy that was cut to make room for me was Brett Hull. The next year he scored 80 goals. He just wasn't into his prime yet.

That was a pretty good time, but it was nowhere near like winning the championship. I still say that the greatest time in my career was winning the Turner Cup with the Detroit Vipers (IHL).

MISSING THE GAME?

Everybody asks me if I miss the game. I say I don't miss it at all. People think I am crazy, but you look back at the 14 years and there is probably one good year out of the whole 14. I had one year that was good for the whole year.

I was in Buffalo that year and everything was going good. I didn't care what was happening, I was playing well and had my family. Other than that it was either Keenan harping on me or worrying about being traded from Buffalo or San Jose. So when people say that they would like to be in my shoes, I say be careful what you ask for, because I use to ask for that too.

Mike Keenan was bad. If I had made it through his tenure there, I would have probably been all right, but once you start getting traded and moving all over, it gets hard. My wife got tired of it, going from Chicago to San Jose to Buffalo. Then we went from Buffalo to New York to Toronto in one year.

Sometimes (as a player) you get labeled. You might say something wrong to one coach. I don't want to say that making it to the NHL is politically driven, because I don't believe that it's out there. I would hate to think that it is.

There are so many guys that I played with in the IHL that should have had a chance, but they never did. Why? Because maybe they weren't at the top of the team's prospects list. They would say, 'Even though he might have had the best training camp but he's not up here on the list, so we aren't going to look at him. Maybe it's an accident that he scored three goals.' That part of it exists.

ELVIS THE ANTAGONIZER

Presley always seemed to be the perfect antagonizer. He seemed to be a natural at getting under the opposition's skin, especially with defensemen and goaltenders. Without saying a word he would take up residency around the net and irritate his foe, many times resulting in his team being the recipient of a power play.

Actually I had that ability my whole career, and didn't even know it. I was out the other day with Carl Liscombe (ex-Red Wing player), he was my coach my first year with Little Caesars'. He said I was even pretty feisty back then, getting under people's skin. I just think it made me who I was in the NHL. It made people hate me.

But, you see it in every sport. It doesn't mean that I am a bad guy. Kirk Maltby is like that. But he does his job and does it well. If players were smart enough they would just do their job and leave him alone. He's not going to do anything, he's not going to score five goals. He's out there to disrupt (Peter) Forsberg, and (Joe) Sakic and whoever. And he does it well. If you focus on just playing and let him be, he's going to get frustrated and end up taking penalties himself."

You have to be born with it, because my son is not. He knows the game, and he has watched it. He was singing the National Anthem since he was two. He knows the game better than any player from his team. He's smart, but he doesn't have the drive, the determination. He's got talent, but maybe he just doesn't have that little burr that gets under people's skin. He might get it, I don't know. But, I think you are born with it.

THE KEENAN YEARS AND CAREER HIGHLIGHTS

While Mike Keenan has had success in the coaching game - winning a Stanley Cup with the New York Rangers in 1994 – most players that have played for him will also tell you how difficult of a coach he is. If he doesn't like you, you know you are on the bubble. Presley played for Keenan in Chicago from 1988, when Keenan arrived, to 1991 when he was sent to San Jose.

When people think back on anything in life, you only think of the good times. You really have to think hard about the bad times. I think I had a great career. If somebody asks me, yea I liked it. I had fun. But then I start thinking about all the times where it wasn't quite as good. I had three bad years under Keenan in Chicago.

We would be on the road and lose a couple of games. In those games I would get maybe four minutes ice time each game. So, we'd come back home and there would be a couple of guys whose gear would be down from their lockers and in another room, and there would be guys that were just called up using your locker. That's how he does stuff.

I was a three or four year veteran and I am changing my gear in the laundry room or the boiler room. So that kind of stuck in my mind. But I also think that him being there kept me in the league longer. I don't want to give him credit, but he made me want to stay in the league longer.

Both playoff runs I had with him were probably the highlights of my NHL career. One time I sat out 18 straight games at the end of the year. I didn't play the first playoff game and we lost to Minnesota 5-2, the next game he inserted myself and Bob Murray in. I scored two goals and we won the game. Then I believe we went on to beat Detroit the next round, and I had a fabulous playoff.

I had two penalty shots at the Boston Gardens. I was the only player to be awarded two in that building. I had one goal and one miss.

The first one I scored was pretty phenomenal. Darren Pang is a good friend of mine. We met at the hotel for a couple of drinks the night before the game. I told him I was going to score that game. It was the end of the season and I wasn't getting much ice time. So I was killing a penalty, had a breakaway on the net and was pulled down and got a penalty shot.

But having those two penalty shots there was special. I think (Derek) Sanderson was the one that told me, 'You know you are the only one to have two here.'

Playing in the league (NHL) is something that I can tell my grandkids. My youngest daughter loved me with the Vipers, and loved all the guys. She was always there. But she doesn't know my NHL career. Just to have my kids have the memories of me playing is the greatest thing. When I am fifty or sixty my son can tell stories about my playing.

RIVALRIES

In hockey, as with any sport, certain teams just have a tendency to develop a rivalry with each other, making their contests much more important - a higher intensity, if you will. This is what brings the fans in droves and provides the players with a little extra incentive to play a game that otherwise may not hold much meaning. Call it bragging rights, call it a rivalry, but it makes the game much more exciting.

We never really had many rivalries. When I was with Chicago we had Detroit, Minnesota and St. Louis. Those three were huge rivalries. Every game we played against them was like a playoff game. Then you would go against other teams and it wouldn't even be close to the intensity of those games. It was like that my whole career in Chicago.

It didn't matter if we had 50 points or 100 points, we'd go into Detroit or St. Louis and it would be a battle. I don't know if I like the way they (the NHL) have changed it around. You're not going to have those anymore. It's gone.

Go to Buffalo and they have Boston, which was always a huge battle. You don't see it anymore. So, what they did was to turn the regular season into just another game, until the playoffs come.

When I was with San Jose, there was nobody. The first year there were no rivalries. It was just a bunch of minor league players, who were just happy to be there. Now they have one with L.A., due to the two teams being so close in proximity.

With the new alignment, they have broken up much of the rivalries. The only ones left are probably New York (Rangers), New York (Islanders), and New Jersey. Other than that, it's gone.

BEST PLAYERS

I played against, and with, a lot of great players. The best I can think of for playing against was probably Mario Lemieux. He was by far the best that I played against. He was so big and strong. You can't hit Gretzky, he's off limits, but if you hit Lemieux, you're going to feel it. He was probably the best in that respect.

Then there was Brian Leetch and Mark Messier. I sort of knew that Messier was as good as he is, but Leetch was great. As far as looking at him play and watching him play, to actually playing with him, there's a gap. I always thought that he was alright, but when I played with him I knew how good he was. You never really realize how good a player is until you play with them.

It just goes to show you how the media can create a star or an award for somebody. I think it's hard for anybody on the West Coast to win any awards. They have to become phenomenal, because the coverage is all in the East.

I never really believed that when I played in Chicago. I didn't really care about what happened out there. I always heard that that was why teams back East win all the awards. They would say it was because all the coverage was back here and in New York. Then when I went out to San Jose, you never heard about the guys back East.

The media sees the players here every game, when I was in San Jose you might see a team from back east for three games.

For those three games Leetch might not play well. You think, 'He's not that good.' But he really is. He's above everybody else.

RETIRING FROM THE NHL

In one season Presley had gone from the Buffalo Sabres to the New York Rangers to the Toronto Maple Leafs. So it was no wonder that when Toronto decided they wanted to send him down to their St. John's (AHL) affiliate at the start of the 1996-97 season, he decided he was tired of moving his family and that it was time to leave the NHL and head home.

Presley came back to Detroit, Michigan, where he was raised, to be with his family in a time of need. It was there that then-Detroit Vipers head coach Steve Ludzik called on Elvis. Ludzik was looking for some high-caliber talent to help his team on their quest for the International Hockey League's Turner Cup. It was the lure of possibly winning the silver chalice that brought Presley back in the game.

Due to my moving around, my kids were always real open to everything. They always had friends. My daughter would go into a new school and make friends the first day.

I was traded to Toronto in February of 1996, and finished that year with them. I think the point (of retirement) came when they said, 'We're going to send you down (to St. John's), and see if you clear waivers.' They said for me to just go home for a couple of days.

I drove the kids to school and I could see in their faces that they were not happy there. It was then that I realized that they had had enough. I said, 'That's it, we're going home today.' They didn't even go to school that day, I went home packed the truck up and we drove it home (to Detroit). When I got home, I contacted Toronto and said that I wanted to discuss a buy out.

I discussed with my family the fact that I might be traded, and if I was going to go. On top of all that, my Grandmother had cancer and there was personal stuff back home. We just decided that it wasn't worth going anywhere else, and that after 14 years, it was better to just go home and be there.

Once we got home, the kids got into school and they loved it. So it was a pretty easy adjustment. People say it was probably hard, but it really wasn't. I come from a pretty big Italian family on my mom's side and we're pretty close. So, with what was going on with my grandmother, everyone wanted to be home.

Ludzy (Detroit Vipers' head coach Steve Ludzik) called me right away when he found out I was bought out. The original plan was for Toronto to pay me and have me play for the Vipers. But, they wanted to get rid of my salary and wouldn't send me there. The buy out didn't happen until December of 1996. After that I started playing with the Vipers.

Playing for the Vipers and winning the Turner Cup[26] was probably the greatest moment in my career. I had 32 goals one year, I played on the U.S. team in the Canada Cup, but I never won a

While league championships eluded Wayne Presley during his 14-year NHL playing career, the hard-nosed right winger became a part of the 1997 Detroit Vipers' (IHL) Turner Cup Championship team. Wayne is seen here with teammates awaiting the presentation of the Trophy.

Photo © 1997 Lawrence P. Nader

---

[26] The Detroit Vipers, in their 4th season of existence, posted a record of 57-17-8 en route to their first ever Turner Cup Championship in the 1996-97 season.

championship. Winning that championship (1997) was an unbelievable feeling. It worked out really well.

I don't know if I was done after that year. You know how minor hockey is, its all dollars. The money wasn't there, so I didn't sign at first. Then they felt that they had another run at the cup in 1998, so they called me back. But, that year wasn't the same as the previous year. Playing there in 1997 was a good transition for me from the NHL. It allowed me to be at home, do what I wanted to do and see my family. It allowed me to see events that my kids were involved in at school. For 14 years I never saw those things, because I was either on the road or had other commitments.

Ludzy ran things pretty easy with me. I told him I wanted to be there because I believed that we were going to win, but I came back to be with my family. If something family related comes up I was going to do it. That made it a lot easier. It was a good time.

AFTER THE GAME

The Vipers didn't win their second consecutive Turner Cup in 1998, losing out in seven games in the Cup Finals to the Chicago Wolves. Presley went on to completely retire from the game after that year, settling into the business world and coaching his son's youth hockey team in Southfield, Michigan.

I got into coaching in 1997 in Southfield. When we came back from Toronto in October of 1996 it was the only organization that had room for him. I called everywhere to try to just get him into a house league and Southfield was the only organization that had room for him. We got him in there and he finished out that year with them.

The coach asked me if I wanted to help out. I never really thought I would like coaching, but it's something that I like doing. It's hard, being that I am coaching my kid. He's not the best kid on the team. He's very good, but not the best. It helps out that I don't show him any special treatment. When we're on a power play, I put my best kids out there, and Michael's (Presley's son) not on the ice.

I really enjoy it, but I don't think that I'll ever get into coaching professionally.

Other than that I am trying to switch careers. I am in the mortgage business. It's pretty difficult, but I like it. The thing I like the best about it, is that it's like a hockey player's schedule. You don't have to be there all day. If I'm there I'm making money and if I'm not there I'm not making money.

I don't know that I'll be there forever, but the mortgage industry is on a high right now, so it's something else on my resume other than hockey. In a year or more, mortgage rates might skyrocket, then I'll move on.

I actually got involved in the business from Jimmy

Wayne Presley catches a breather during the International Hockey League's 1997 Turner Cup Playoffs.
Photo © 1997 Lawrence P. Nader

Carson. I called him up to ask if he knew of anyone looking for help, and he landed this position for me. If it's a year, or two years, or whatever, I'll have something else on my resume.

I had a couple of offers through my agent Larry Kelly, he represents Steve Yzerman, and he's talking about branching out in the Detroit area. I had a couple of discussions with him about that. So I might do that, but I don't know. I don't much enjoy watching hockey anymore. The only time I watch it on TV anymore is if someone I like is playing. I don't care about any of the guys I played with in the NHL. I like to watch the guys I played with in the IHL, that are getting a chance in the NHL. These guys are getting a chance that I wish more of them would get. I enjoy watching them.

But, as for my future, I don't know what's out there.

WAYNE PRESLEY'S CAREER STATS

Season	Team	League	GP	G	A	Pts	PIM
1982-83	Kitchener Rangers	OHL	70	39	48	87	99
1983-84	Kitchener Rangers	OHL	70	63	76	139	156
1984-85	Chicago Blackhawks	NHL	3	0	1	1	0
1984-85	Kitchener Rangers	OHL	31	25	21	46	77
1984-85	Sault Ste. Marie Greyhounds	OHL	11	5	9	14	14
1985-86	Nova Scotia Oilers	AHL	29	6	9	15	22
1985-86	Chicago Blackhawks	NHL	38	7	8	15	38
1986-87	Chicago Blackhawks	NHL	80	32	29	61	114
1987-88	Chicago Blackhawks	NHL	42	12	10	22	52
1988-89	Chicago Blackhawks	NHL	72	21	19	40	100
1989-90	Chicago Blackhawks	NHL	49	6	7	13	69
1990-91	Chicago Black Hawks	NHL	71	15	19	34	122
1991-92	San Jose Sharks	NHL	47	8	14	22	76
1991-92	Buffalo Sabres	NHL	12	2	2	4	57

WAYNE PRESLEY'S CAREER STATS
(CONT.)

Season	Team	League	GP	G	A	Pts	PIM
1992-93	Buffalo Sabres	NHL	79	15	17	32	96
1993-94	Buffalo Sabres	NHL	65	17	8	25	103
1994-95	Buffalo Sabres	NHL	46	14	5	19	41
1995-96	Toronto Maple Leafs	NHL	19	2	2	4	14
1996-97	St. Johns Maple Leafs	AHL	2	0	0	0	0
1996-97	Detroit Vipers	IHL	42	7	16	23	80
1997-98	Detroit Vipers	IHL	16	1	5	6	47
	NHL Totals		**684**	**155**	**147**	**302**	**953**

Johnny Wilson

NHL Career: 1949-1962 (12 seasons)
NHL Teams: Detroit Red Wings, Chicago Black Hawks, Toronto Maple Leafs, New York Rangers

Johnny Wilson broke into the NHL with the Detroit Red Wings in the 1949-1950 season and wore the winged wheel crest until 1955 when he was part of a 7-man trade with the Chicago Blackhawks. The deal sent Wilson, Tony Leswick, Glen Skov and Benny Woit to the Windy City in return for Dave Creighton, Bucky Hollingsworth and Jerry Toppazzinni. The move was short lived as in 1957 the Blackhawks sent Hank Bessen, Forbes Kennedy, Wilson and Bill Preston to the Motor City receiving Glenn Hall and Ted Lindsay in trade.

In addition to Detroit (where he remained until 1959) and Chicago, Wilson also played for the Toronto Maple Leafs and New York Rangers during his 12-year National Hockey League career. He was a member of Detroit's 1950, 52, 54 & 55 championship teams and also coached the Red Wings from the final 67 games of the 1971-72 season through the end of the 1972-73 season, carrying a 67-56-22 record.

Besides coaching Detroit, Wilson also coached the World Hockey Association's (WHA) Michigan Stags, Baltimore Blades and Cleveland Crusaders, and the NHL's Los Angeles Kings, Colorado Rockies and Pittsburgh Penguins.

BREAKING INTO THE NHL

Johnny Wilson played his junior days across the river from Detroit in Windsor, Ontario where he played for the Windsor Hettche Spitfires of the International Hockey League from 1947-49. He not only remembers how impressed he was to go to

Detroit's Olympia Stadium and watch the names he grew up admiring, but he also remembers those same players coming to Windsor to watch their junior games. He remembers the advice they provided, which helped him and others on their way to the NHL.

My junior days were spent in Windsor. In those days the Red Wings sponsored and owned the junior players on the team. It was like a farm team for the Red Wings. They don't have that structure today. We competed against one another on the team to turn pro and develop in the Red Wing organization.

We were fortunate here in Detroit as junior players, we lived in Windsor and we got passes or free admission to see the Red Wings play on Sunday nights. That kind of enhanced your development because you could actually see what was transpiring on the ice, and you'd sort of pattern yourself after a player. My idol at that time was Ted Lindsay, not knowing that two years after juniors I'd be playing on the same team with him.

Ted and Gordie Howe use to come over and watch us play on Saturday nights when they were off. They kind of gave you a little boost in terms of your professional career, which you could see down the road. They were driving big cars and we were walking. To play professionally and make some (at that time) big money, was a major goal in life. We (the team) developed together. My brother (Larry Wilson), four other guys from that team and myself ended up turning pro.

We went from there to Omaha, which was the chain. They would give you a year or two down there and if you didn't develop to their specifications they probably let you go or trade you. The next step, if you had a good year, was that you played in Indianapolis. They developed you slowly.

Once you played in Indianapolis and Omaha, you went to training camp and were a candidate to play with the Wings. Naturally you had to dislodge somebody from the parent team to move in. Most of the time the guy you bumped was up in his early thirties or late twenties, so they'd move the old guy out or make a deal. In my era, rookies broke in maybe once every two, or four years.

I had good years with Omaha and Indianapolis and made it up to Detroit but they didn't think I was ready. They gave me about a month and a half with the team and then sent me back to Indianapolis to get some more playing time. When I got back to Indianapolis I got hot and started scoring some goals, so they called me back up. That was the last of my time in the minors."

As a rookie, walking into the dressing room and seeing the likes of Lindsay, Howe, Sid Abel and Jack Stewart that was a big thrill for me. You'd sit back, pay attention, and keep your mouth shut and listen.

Ted Lindsay and Sid Abel were good captains. They would sit down with the rookies and work with them. They would enlighten them in what to expect and sort of give you a fast education in what the National Hockey League is all about. If you needed any help or assistance, Lindsay was there. You didn't have to knock on his door, he was right there for you.

THE NORRIS' – JAMES, MARGUERITE AND BRUCE

The Red Wings were owned by the Norris family from 1932 until 1982, and was operated by various members of the family during Wilson's time with the organization. From the days of James Norris Sr. all the way through Marguerite and Bruce Norris, Wilson saw it all as a player and coach. While the Norris' served as owners, it was the legendary Jack Adams who assembled a team that was arguably one of the best teams ever to be iced in the NHL.

I go back to the days of the eldest Norris, Mr. (James) Norris. We use to call him the old man. But he maintained his home in Chicago, not Detroit. When I was a kid he would come to training camp and he had a fabulous memory. Jack Adams would take him around and introduce him to all the players. He'd come back the next day and he would know each player by his name. He knew what you looked like and he wouldn't call you Jimmy instead of John.

We never saw much of James Norris though. Jack Adams ran the team. Then, in the 1952 season, Marguerite Norris[27] stepped up and became the President until 1955, the last year we won the cup. Then Bruce Norris sort of moved in.

Jack Adams ran the organization, you didn't hear too much from the Norris'. Jack ran things for the old man, Jim, and Marguerite. But, when Bruce came in, I don't know if it was Adams' age or what, but finally they let Jack go[28].

In my opinion, the Norris' were absentee owners. You didn't see much of them. Of course, as a player, you don't mind because you feel that owners are more critical. When you have local ownership, like the Ilitches (Mike Ilitch bought the team from Bruce Norris in 1982), you have instant answers. You don't have to track a guy down that maybe went to Europe or went here or there. They're involved. If Mike Ilitch had been an absentee owner, they wouldn't have been as successful as they have been.

The Norris' were going down the tubes because they lost control. What destroyed the Red Wings dynasty, was that the Chicago Blackhawks, which the Norris' also owned, were hurting at the box office and they didn't have the farm team and structure to the organization that the Red Wings had.

So what was the result? The Norris' would call-up Jack and say, 'Oh Jack we need some help.' Jack would say, 'I've got two or three young kids that are going to help you, but I need such and such in return.' 'No Problem.' That's how they destroyed this club.

We could have won three or four more Stanley Cups, all in the late 50's and maybe the early 60's had we maintained the same hockey players. There was a fever on the team that we had to win. We were proud of the organization, proud of Detroit. I

---

[27] Marguerite Norris, the daughter of James Norris Sr., took over as President for the Red Wings in 1952 following her father's death. She remained in the position until replaced by her brother Bruce in 1955.

[28] Jack Adams served as the Red Wings' general manager from the team's second season (1927-28) through the end of the 1962-63 campaign when he was replaced by Ex-Red Wing Sid Abel.

don't care who you are, you have to be fortunate to play here (Detroit). Kiss the ground you're standing on because this is the best city in the world, from the way I feel.

DRINKING FROM THE CUP – FOUR TIMES OVER

During his career, Wilson had the honor of celebrating a Stanley Cup Championship on four separate occasions – each time was with the Red Wings during their 1950's dynasty years.[29] Wilson reflects on those special moments in his life.

The first time you win the Stanley Cup is something that every young hockey player dreams of. Unfortunately, everybody that plays hockey doesn't have that opportunity to win it. Fortunately,

Left Wing Johnny Wilson enjoyed Stanley Cup Championship seasons with the Detroit Red Wings in 1950, 1952, 1954 and 1955. Wilson played in 688 NHL games with four teams – Detroit Red Wings, Chicago Blackhawks, Toronto Maple Leafs and New York Rangers) earning 332 points (161-171) and 190 penalty minutes.

Photo © 1998 Lawrence P. Nader

---

[29] The Detroit Red Wings were on fire in the 1950's winning the Stanley Cup four times (1950, 1952, 1954, and 1955). Only the legendary Montreal Canadiens were better winning five times during the decade (1953, 1956, 1957, 1958 and 1959). The Toronto Maple Leafs won the other Cup in 1951.

for me, I was associated with the Red Wings at the time that they were putting a dynasty together.

When you win the first Cup you kind of take a back seat. You look at everything else around you and the stars are hoisting the cup. In those days you couldn't lift the cup over your head like today. You had the base and then the Cup, it was in two parts. Back then we were presented with the original Stanley Cup which is the one in the Hockey Hall of Fame in Toronto.

Today teams are presented with the replica Cup, so they can drop it, throw it, or do what ever they want with it. It's all one piece now so you can grab it and lift it up.

It was a great thrill, as a player, to win the Cup. But after you won it, you only had a short period of time to cherish it before you never saw it again. It was a very coveted piece of silverware. Back then, you were presented with it on the ice and celebrated with it in the dressing room and that was the end of it until you won it the next year.

Today, they get to take the replica all over. They put kids in it, throw it in the swimming pool, take it fishing and do whatever they want to with it in the couple of days that each player gets to have it.

It was fun playing on those teams. It's always nice to go into a season knowing you have an excellent opportunity to win. We had some great hockey clubs then. We had some well-balanced lines, solid defense and great goaltending. Similar to what the Red Wings have today (late 1990's). Everybody on those teams contributed in terms of winning the Cup.

I remember in 1952 when we won the Cup in 8 straight games, I got hot against Toronto in the semi-finals and had a couple of winning goals. I also got a winning goal against Montreal in the Stanley Cup finals. So of the eight games, I scored the winning goal in three of them. Back then we only had three lines. Today they have four lines plus a couple of extra forwards. We only dressed 17 players – 11 forwards, 5 defensemen and 1 goaltender. So when your big players, guys like Howe and Lindsay, were being shadowed by the opposition, it was important for the rest of us to come through.

Everybody has their own ways of celebrating and cherishing the Cup when they win it. I think over the years, it has become even more cherished. To win it today is even bigger than when we won it. Back then there were no parades. The only parade we were given went from center ice to the dressing room.

I had the pleasure of being asked to ride in a float when the Red Wings won the Cup in 1997 and 1998. It was one of the greatest thrills I ever had. When we pulled out from the parking lot at the Fox Theater and looked towards Downtown Detroit all you saw was tons and tons of people all the way to the waterfront. They were stacked. There was just enough room for the procession to go through.

In the days when we played, the only parade they had was for the Yankees when they won the World Series. They had a ticker tape parade on Wall Street. We didn't have that pleasure, today they do.

They also get to take the Stanley Cup home today so that they can celebrate it with their friends and family for a couple of days each. I think that is a nice tribute to their hard work and winning the Cup. Also, we didn't have the exposure and media coverage that they have today when we won the Stanley Cup.

We were a very close club the years we won. I think that was due to us traveling by train all the time. We spent a lot of hours together on those road trips. We had 4 or 5-day trips every second week or so. Occasionally we had the short run to Chicago to Toronto, but mostly when we headed east we would play Montreal, Boston and New York. As a result we spent a lot of hours on the train. We would walk around and visit each other, go and have lunch together and then come back to our seating area. It really brought us close together as a team.

I still say that Detroit is the greatest city in all of hockey to play in. I played in Toronto, Chicago and New York as well, and while Toronto is on the same wavelength as Detroit with hockey, the fans here (Detroit) really put their athletes on a pedestal. It makes a player feel good. It makes you want to produce and win for the city and the fans. It really jacks you up.

CHICAGO DAYS

As it is in the hockey world, players get traded. Sometimes it is at the players urging, and other times it comes as a total surprise. According to Wilson, it only hurts badly the first time.

Being traded my first time was to Chicago. I was being traded from a championship team. In our era, we developed with the Red Wings and you belonged to the Wings since you were 17 years old. So when you're traded it kinds of hurts. It's disappointing because you feel like you're growing in the organization. You worked hard, and you feel a strong bond.

The second time I was traded, after two years or so, it doesn't mean as much. You're not as disappointed. You say, 'okay it's part of the business.' But the first time was very difficult."

Wilson only stayed in Chicago for two seasons before he was dealt back to Detroit. The 1957 trade saw Wilson, Hank Bassen, Forbes Kennedy and Bill Preston sent to Detroit in exchange for banished goaltender Glen Hall and ex-team captain Ted Lindsay.

Jack Adams sent Hall packing after the two increased their feud that developed when Trader Jack blamed Hall for the Wings playoff failure the previous year when Montreal defeated Detroit 4 games to 1 in the Stanley Cup Finals.

Lindsay, meanwhile, was banished from the Red Wings system by Adams and Bruce Norris in retaliation for his part in attempting to organize a players association. Wilson remembers his days in the Windy City.

I had a couple of great years in Chicago. I played there with (Ed) Litzenberger and (Eric) Nesterenko. One of my years there we were the second highest scoring line in the National Hockey League. We were behind the Montreal line of Dickie Moore, Maurice (Rocket) Richard and Henri (Pocket Rocket) Richard.

At the time that I arrived in Chicago, they were rebuilding the team after hitting rock bottom. The league was trying to help the Blackhawks and, even more, so was Detroit because the Norris family owned both teams. Since Detroit had an abundance of hockey players, they tried to boost Chicago. Back in the 1950's when the Wings were winning the Stanley Cup, their farm teams Indianapolis and Omaha were winning their respective Cups. In addition, their junior team in Windsor was winning the OHA championship. So they had a lot of great players in their system – a lot of depth. Chicago didn't have that depth. So Detroit would slide their players to the Blackhawks in hope of building the team up.

I was only there for two years, but I had a lot of fun. Chicago Stadium had a lot of character and the fans there went bananas. When I was in Detroit there was a number of places where we could skate and practice since a lot of hockey was played in the area. Back then in Chicago, if we didn't have ice at Chicago Stadium we had to travel 30 or 40 miles out of town in order to practice.

Unlike in Detroit, when you walked out of the Stadium in Chicago, no one knew you from a bale of hay. At that time, in the late 1950's, television was just starting to surface and then you could be identified because we didn't wear helmets.

While the fans in Chicago would cheer us, we really had nothing to strive for. Every game was a struggle since we didn't have the personnel to compete. When I was in Detroit we always had the personnel we needed and the fans would rally behind your efforts. You can't blame the Chicago fans, they cheered hard but they had nothing to grab onto. We'd win 15 to 20 games a year out of 70. We just kind of hung in there.

It was discouraging there because football and baseball dominated the newspapers at that time. Hockey had some coverage but nothing like in Detroit. In Detroit you would make the headlines in the sports section. It was always a boost to see you name in the headlines, but in Chicago the stories were buried inside the sports section. They were usually small articles and, as a result, you feel like you were not appreciated.

Plus the sports writers there were not as knowledgeable about hockey as they were in Detroit. In Detroit they had some big sports writers like John Walters and Joe Falls who really knew the game. But in Chicago, you didn't know half of the writers and they wouldn't give you much exposure. So you were kind of lost in the Windy City.

THE MAPLE LEAFS

Following the 1958-59 season with Detroit, Wilson was sent packing once again – this time to Toronto and the historic Maple Leaf Gardens. In the summer of 1959 Wilson was traded to the Leafs in exchange for right wing Barry Cullen. Even though the fans in Toronto always booed and jeered Wilson when he came into town with an opposing team, once he put on the white and blue Maple Leafs jersey all that changed.

When I left the Red Wings and headed to Toronto, things were starting to get tough in Detroit. They were starting to sputter. Lindsay had retired and there were a lot of players that Jack Adams felt were getting long in the tooth. Things weren't going that well so he traded a lot of players. Being traded to Toronto shed new light on my career. Punch Imlach was a different type of coach, he let you play your own game. On top of that we were contenders. I enjoyed it in Toronto. I scored a lot of important goals for them that year.

One of the great things about Toronto was Saturday night hockey. The fans really got fired up for that and they took me right in. Anytime you play for the home team, they forget what you did when you were the opposition. All of a sudden you have their Maple Leaf sweater on and they are in your corner cheering you one all the way.

The Montreal Canadiens and Toronto Maple Leafs were a most viscous rivalry. They were the only two Canadien cities playing in the National League and they always played hard fought games against each other. The other rivalries in the league did not compare to those two teams. Detroit and Toronto, while it was always a great rivalry, was not even close. The intensity was much higher. The media even got in on it with the French and English media taking shots both ways.

When you traveled into Montreal, the fans really supported their Canadiens and they left you hear it. Likewise, the fans in Toronto would give the Canadiens a hard time. When Toronto played Montreal you had to win. It was imperative that you didn't lose to Montreal, and because of that we really had some viscous battles. We had Johnny Bower in net for us and Jacques Plante was at the other end for Montreal. We had some great 2-1 and 1-0 games and one night, before we had overtime, we played to a 0-0 tie.

You had to win against the Canadiens when Punch Imlach was coaching. You could lose to Chicago by a goal, but not to Montreal. I remember we were playing one night on a Thursday in Montreal and we lost the game in the last five minutes. We should have won that night.

We left Montreal by train about 11:00 p.m. and got back in Toronto around 7:00 a.m. Normally after you played a game and traveled all night, they wouldn't make you practice that day. Punch was so mad that he told us all to stay downtown because he wanted to practice at 11:00 a.m.

If we had lost against Detroit or Chicago he wouldn't have said a word, but because we lost to Montreal he took the whip out. He worked us hard that day because we were playing the Canadiens in Toronto on Saturday and he wanted to send a message to us. We made sure that we won the game on Saturday.

We played Montreal in the finals that year (59-60) after eliminating Detroit 4 games to 2 to get there. The Canadiens had eliminated Boston and they had a slight edge on us in terms of horsepower. They defeated us in four straight games that year, but I got to see the Rocket score his last goal in the NHL that year. He came down on the right side, went around the net and fired a backhand into the top corner.

The next year we went to camp and several of us had problems with our contracts. We had found out that Montreal was getting paid a lot more per player than the Leafs, so we all put a front up to try to get more money. In those days $1,000 was a big raise. If you asked for $2,000 they would send you out of town.

Opening game that year was in Montreal on a Thursday night and Punch Imlach said, 'To hell with you guys. I'm going to take some minor league players and I'll show you guys that you are not that important to this club. He went to Montreal with the minor league players and they got blown out something like 7-2. The next night they went into Boston and were blown out again.

I was working out with the Windsor Bulldogs to stay in shape as I sat out for a couple of weeks. Finally King Clancy called me and said to come back. He said that he knew I was in condition but that they wanted me to play in Rochester (Toronto's farm team) for the weekend. I played two games down there and scored 4 points (2goals, 2 assists). After that I came back to Toronto.

ENDING IT IN NEW YORK

After playing just three games following his return to the Maple Leafs, Wilson was traded to the New York Rangers for Eddie Shack. Shack was in the doghouse at the time and the Rangers were looking to move him elsewhere.

Wilson played two seasons with the Rangers before deciding to retire following the 1961-62 season. He figured his time had come and he had a good job offer that provided a solid year round income that would help him better provide for his growing family. Expansion was still a few years off. Had it come earlier, it might have prolonged Wilson's career for a number of years like it did for many other stars of that era.

I retired with the Rangers in 1962. I could have stayed longer but I had an offer of a permanent job with Molson Brewery of Canada. I had been representing them in the summers during my playing days, and they wanted me to quit hockey to take a job with them permanently. My family was starting to grow and it was time to put them in school and I knew I wasn't going to stay in New York the rest of my life.

New York was a tough place to play because you traveled a lot and you didn't have the luxuries you had here in Detroit.

You never practice at the Gardens and if you did it was upstairs on the fifth floor. The rink up there was odd shaped because one end had a restaurant that took away from the ice and it had aluminum boards. The puck didn't bounce off of them well. In Detroit we always practiced at the Olympia, we very seldom practiced anyplace else. The arena was a second home.

We lived on Long Island and it would take a good hour and twenty minutes to get to the Gardens. It also cost us for parking, since the Gardens didn't own the parking lot. Plus you had to cross three or four tunnels to get downtown and babysitting was a buck-ten an hour. Back in Detroit it was 35 cents. When you put all this together, it would cost you a lot just to go play hockey.

But I had a good year in the 1961-62 season. It was the first time New York had been in the playoffs for years. I broke in Rod Gilbert and Jean Ratelle that season and we almost beat Toronto in the playoffs.

Once the season ended, I took the job with Molson and stayed with them. They (the Rangers) called me to go back the following year and the year after. They always thought I would miss the game and return.

Had I stayed for two more years, I would have put another six years on my career with the expansion. That's how guys like Alex (Delvecchio), Gordie (Howe) and others extended their careers. The teams really needed players and a lot of those guys played another six years, or more, because they didn't have enough players to go around.

However, I had a solid job offer and that was important to me. I was locked in with good pay, pensions, a company car, profit sharing, bonuses, expense accounts and insurance. Everything I never had playing hockey. I was also making more money than ever I did playing hockey.

ON COACHING

After a number of years with Molson, Wilson did miss the game and decided to get back into as a coach. He started his coaching career at Princeton University before getting an offer from the Los Angeles Kings to coach in their system. Following the Kings, Wilson took over the bench reigns with Detroit before moving on to coach Michigan, Baltimore and Cleveland in the WHA. After his departure from the faltering WHA, he re-entered the NHL coaching ranks in Colorado and then Pittsburgh.

Coaching is a heck of a lot different than playing. When you are playing, you look at things as an individual performance and trying to blend it in with the team effort. Where as when you are coaching, you are responsible for 18 players. If they don't perform to expectations, all the blame falls on you. Just when you think things are going great, you run into stumbling blocks, and injuries. Being a player is definitely a lot easier than being a coach.

I started out coaching at Princeton University for a couple of years and then the L.A. Kings lured me away. That was how I started coaching in the National League.

My first year with Los Angeles I was sent to Springfield to coach their AHL team which they had recently bought from Eddie Shore. Shore was still around and although he had no association with the team, he continued to operate the arena. All those stories you hear about him are true. When Eddie was mad at me he called me Mr. Wilson. When he was happy he called me Cowboy.

One night he calls me up at 3 A.M. and says, 'Mr. Wilson." I knew that was trouble right from the start. He then told me, 'Your trainer left the light on in the dressing room and it so happens, Mr. Wilson, that I am paying the electric bills.' I told him that I would appreciate it very much if he would turn the light switch off. He said, 'No. I want your trainer down here to turn it off.'

I told him that I would call Bill Burnett, our trainer. Shore hated Burnett with a passion. So I called Bill up at three in the morning and told him, 'Bill, you left the lights on.' He had spent the better part of the night in the bar and was asleep when I called. In his state he said, 'No I didn't. The light's are off.' I said, 'No Bill. The lights in the dressing room.'

I told him that the old man, which is what we referred to Shore as, was in the dressing room and that he better get his ass down there since Shore wasn't going to leave the building until he turned the light off. So he dressed, went to the arena in the middle of the night and turned the lights off. But that was how Shore was. He was a beauty.

One day we were practicing at the arena. I use to try to hold our practices early so that we would be out of the arena before Eddie arrived at 11 o'clock. This one-day something had happened and we had to practice later than usual and started practice at eleven. We asked Teddy Shore, Eddie's son, if that was okay. He checked with the old man and said that it was not a problem.

We were on the ice that day and out of the corner of my eye I see Eddie walk into the building and head into his office. We were warming up and guys were shooting the puck off the glass and the boards, when I saw Eddie walking back around the boards and into the penalty box. All of a sudden I hear the P.A. system go on. He had a record on and you couldn't hear a thing. I was yelling at the players and they couldn't hear me. He had the volume up so loud that the building was trembling.

I figured he was just checking out the sound system so I told the players to waltz around the ice to the music, which they did. Then the old man takes off up the stairs. I figured he was just going to the furthest corner to see if the sound was clear. In the corner upstairs he had his own driving range. So he turns around and sees us skating around and having fun and then goes over there and starts to hit golf balls. I waited about another ten minutes and called the guys into the corner and told them to cancel the practice.

After that I went up to Teddy and asked what the old man was doing. He told me that he would check with Eddie. The next day I come into practice and he told me that when the old man went into his office that day, he got a phone call from a friend of his. With all the shooting and banging, he couldn't hear his friend on the phone. So he said to his friend, 'If I can't hear you, the players are not going to hear the coach.' He was really unbelievable.

After Los Angeles I coached the Red Wings for a couple of years starting midway through the 1970-71 season. That was during the 'Darkness with Harkness'[30] era. It was a terrible time. In those days we had two divisions (East and West). The East division had five of the original six teams and the West division was all expansion teams expect for Chicago. As a result, the East division was a tougher division to play in.

We finished with 86 points in our division and didn't make the playoffs. Meanwhile, teams in the West were making the playoffs with 20 fewer points than us. A year or so after I left Detroit, the NHL changed the format going to a two conference league with two divisions in each conference. Had the format been changed earlier I would have probably coached longer in Detroit.

Harkness and I didn't see eye to eye on a lot of things. We clashed when he coached at Cornell and I was coaching Princeton and things weren't any better between us in Detroit. He was fired as coach of Detroit after 38 games in the 70-71 season and made the team's General Manager. That was when I came in to coach. He wanted to manage and coach the team through me. The players detect that and you lose credibility. That was one thing that I established with the players right away and Harkness didn't like that.

After being fired as coach of the Red Wings in 1973, Wilson took the coaching job for the short-lived Michigan Stags (who were the Los Angeles Sharks the previous season) at the start of the 1974-75 season. About midway through the season, a bankrupt Stags organization pulled up stakes and completed their season in Baltimore before folding for good. Wilson then

---

[30] Ned Harkness' rule as general manager of the Detroit Red Wings, which lasted from the last 40 games of the 1970-71 season through the end of the 1973-74 campaign, was referred to as the "Darkness With Harkness" era. The buzz-phrase emphasized the trouble the Detroit franchise had in maintaining any stability with Harkness at the controls, and the unhappiness experienced by players, coaches and fans.

went on to coach the Cleveland Crusaders before heading to the NHL.

The World Hockey Association, that was quit an experience. My first experience in the World Hockey Association was as coach of the Michigan Stags. In a year's time they went from being the Los Angeles Sharks to the Michigan Stags to the Baltimore Blades.

The reason why the Stags moved is that they ran out of money. The owners had about $5 or $6 million dollars to start the team, which was more than enough. However, when they moved the team here from LA, players demanded advance salary in their contracts. They (the players) wanted to buy houses, so somebody authorized the advancements. Then they (the team) went into a big advertising campaign, in which they were ill advised. All of a sudden that $6 million dollars drained down to nothing. So they moved to Baltimore.

Baltimore wasn't any better financially healed then we were. I went down there and heard the owners screaming 'I ain't giving no half a million dollars.' I thought to myself 'What am I doing here in Baltimore when I just left a team that was in financial distress in Detroit.' I finished the year and that was the end of it.

The next year I went to Cleveland and they were running out of money as well. They went into receivership and eventually disbanded. I wanted to get back into the National Hockey League because World Hockey was kind of shaky at the time. The timing was bad.

The following season (1976-77) the Kansas City Scouts (NHL) were moving the team to Denver where they became the Rockies and they were looking for a head coach. I called them on a Friday to talk with Muncie Campbell and was told that he was in a meeting but they would try to locate him.

Muncie picked up the phone and said that he was in a meeting with other management members of the team and they were discussing who their new head coach would be. I told him I wanted to drop my name in the hat. He said they were just going over the list but would add my name to it and they would have a press conference on Tuesday. I guess I just got in under the wire. Muncie called me Saturday morning and told me to get my bags packed and fly out, that I had the job. I signed a one-year deal with Colorado.

The Rockies' owner Jack Vickers, who was an oil tycoon and a billionaire, was invested in the team with Muncie and Bud Palmer, who used to play Basketball for the New York Knicks and they had moved the team to Denver. That first year we would only really get the crowds when Detroit or Philadelphia would come to town. It was predominately a young city and they (Denver's residents) went skiing on the weekends, not to hockey games.

Jack Vickers owned all the Vickers Gas Stations in town so when you bought ten dollars or so of gas you got two tickets to a hockey game. They tried to get people into the games and stimulate interest. As the year progressed, Vickers had a meeting with all the management and said that he wanted to have some of the players to stay in Denver over the summer and do some canvassing, selling program ads and other promotions. At that time, most of the players went back to Canada during the summer because they didn't have green cards so those plans fell by the wayside.

Following the season Vickers said 'I'll give you one more year, but when I drill for oil and I come back dry, I don't drill in the same area again.' With that in mind, there were rumors that the team might move to Winnipeg, or another place. I had made up my mind that I wasn't going to run from one city to another.

At that point Pittsburgh offered me a long-term contract. I went back to Colorado and they asked me to stick around for one more year, but that was all they were offering me. I told them to offer me a three-year deal like I had in Pittsburgh and I would stay. They didn't want to do that. They wanted to give me one year at a time. So I left and went to Pittsburgh.

After three seasons in Pittsburgh, I left coaching in 1980 and moved back to Detroit.

JOHNNY WILSON TODAY

Even though he is retired from the game itself, Wilson remains active in the Detroit community with his job and his time playing with the Red Wings Alumni in charity games. Wilson remains approachable by the fans and takes time to talk with them whether it be during breaks in a Alumni game, at a local ice rink or while attending Red Wings hockey games at Joe Louis Arena.

I'm enjoying retirement. I play a lot of hockey with the (Red Wing) Alumni, which I've enjoy. I am also a past-President of the Alumni. We take a winter vacation and go to Florida and play a little golf with the guys. We're a very close knit organization. We do a lot for charity around town, which I also enjoy.

I've had my pleasures of fame and coaching. However, careers come to an end, especially in sports. It doesn't go on for eternity. Very few coaches hang tough until they're sixty. Being a coach now, the way I see, after four or five years they get you out of there. They want a change.

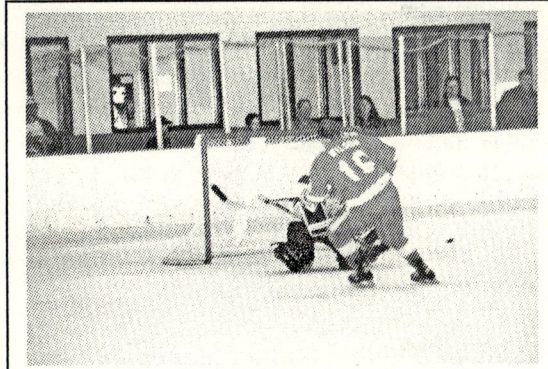

Johnny Wilson is stopped by the opposing goaltender on a breakaway during an Alumni charity game.
Photo © 1998 Lawrence P. Nader

Look at the career that Scotty Bowman has had – St. Louis, Buffalo, Pittsburgh, Montreal and Detroit. Not even Al Arbour has stayed in one place. Sometimes it doesn't matter how good you are. Sometimes you coach a bad team. I use to say to some of the writers, 'Even God couldn't coach this team.'

Owners and management today always think they've got a competitive team. But when you are working with the players you see things that you don't see on the surface. When I watch the Wings now, I see things but I don't see it as a coach, because I'm not working them on a daily basis. I don't see the internal problems.

When the time came along (to quit coaching), I knew to bale out. I wanted to get a permanent job where I could enjoy life, where I could sit down and not have to worry about winning a game tonight. You sort of put yourself in a shell (coaching) and you miss a lot with your family.

Right now, I work and there is always a little pressure but not the kind of pressure that you take home and worry about. The company I work for, Rite-On Industries (Redford, MI) has been just great to me. They made a new life for me. It's something that I enjoy. This job keeps me in touch with everybody in the city. I love doing that.

I mingle with people and make sure they enjoy the game of hockey and even though I'm not playing or coaching, I'm still selling the game. Like a behind the scenes type of thing. I really enjoy seeing the fans and I get asked, 'Johnny, what do you think about this guy?' That's a boost to the organization and people enjoy seeing you there.

JOHNNY WILSON'S CAREER STATS

Season	Team	League	GP	G	A	Pts	PIM
1947-48	Windsor Hettche Spitfires	IHL	25	21	13	34	19
1948-49	Windsor Hettche Spitfires	IHL	4	5	4	9	0
1949-50	Omaha Knights	USHL	70	41	39	80	46
1949-50	Detroit Red Wings	NHL	1	0	0	0	0
1950-51	Indianapolis Capitals	AHL	70	34	21	55	48
1951-52	Indianapolis Capitals	AHL	42	25	14	39	16
1951-52	Detroit Red Wings	NHL	28	4	5	9	18
1952-53	Detroit Red Wings	NHL	70	23	19	42	22
1953-54	Detroit Red Wings	NHL	70	17	17	34	22
1954-55	Detroit Red Wings	NHL	70	12	15	27	14
1955-56	Chicago Blackhawks	NHL	70	24	9	33	12
1956-57	Chicago Blackhawks	NHL	70	18	30	48	24
1957-58	Detroit Red Wings	NHL	70	12	27	39	14
1958-59	Detroit Red Wings	NHL	70	11	17	28	18
1959-60	Toronto Maple Leafs	NHL	70	15	16	31	8

JOHNNY WILSON'S CAREER STATS
(CONT.)

Season	Team	League	GP	G	A	Pts	PIM
1960-61	Rochester Americans	AHL	2	2	2	4	0
1960-61	New York Rangers	NHL	56	14	12	26	24
1960-61	Toronto Maple Leafs	NHL	3	0	1	1	0
1961-62	New York Rangers	NHL	40	11	3	14	14
	NHL Totals		**688**	**161**	**171**	**332**	**190**

JOHNNY WILSON'S NHL COACHING RECORD

Season	Team	G	W	L	T	%
1969-70	Los Angeles Kings	52	9	34	9	.260
1971-73	Detroit Red Wings	145	67	56	22	.538
1976-77	Colorado Rockies	80	20	46	14	.338
1977-80	Pittsburgh Penguins	240	91	105	44	.471
	NHL Totals	**517**	**187**	**241**	**89**	**.448**

About The Author

Born on October 7, 1958 in Detroit, Michigan, Larry Nader started playing and following the game of hockey at the age of 12. Despite the Red Wings being a shell of their former selves at that time, Nader found a love for the game in his hometown team.

In addition to closely following the Red Wings, and developing an attachment to the Montreal Canadiens, as did most hockey fans during that era, he loved watching the rivalries with nearby teams like Toronto and Chicago.

Joining the United States Navy in 1976, Nader was afforded the opportunity to watch minor professional hockey for the first time while stationed in Virginia Beach, VA, when nearby Hampton Roads placed a short lived team in the American Hockey League in the mid 1970's.

After spending nearly a year on the Pacific Island of Guam, his ship was assigned to the shipyards in Long Beach, CA, where Nader was able to attend several LA Kings games, including a preseason contest (September 1979) against the Edmonton Oilers in their first season with the NHL. Featured for the Oilers that day was the hard to miss phenom Wayne Gretzky who, despite his young age, was already gaining worldwide acclaim.

Upon being discharge from the military in 1982, Nader returned to his home in Detroit and began following the Red Wings once again, while discovering the excitement of junior 'A' hockey across the Canadian Border in Windsor, Ontario.

When the Ontario Hockey League placed a franchise in Detroit for the start of the 1990-91 season, Nader became a season ticket holder and eventually assumed the position of Vice President for the team's booster club before moving on to become the founding president of the International Hockey League's Detroit Vipers Fan(g) Club in their inaugural season (1994-95).

In 1996, Nader started a monthly magazine called Great Lakes Hockey Alliance in which he published a column called Tales From The Rink. These columns provided his readers with insight into the player's career and life before and after their National Hockey League days. From these articles, Nader began to compile this book by the same name.

Today, Nader continues to live in the Detroit area with his wife Janis while interviewing players for additional books in the Tales From The Rink series. He also keeps active covering the Detroit Vipers for an Internet magazine (www.inthecrease.com) and providing the team (Vipers) with game reports.